Timely Insights
Into
Timeless Truth

Kenneth J. Brown

Authentic Publishing
129 Mobilization Drive, Waynesboro, GA 30830, USA authenticusa@stl.org
and 9 Holdom Avenue, Bletchley, Milton Keynes, Bucks, MK1 1QR, UK

Cover design by Paul Lewis

Printed in the United States of America

Dedication

To my wife, Margie, and my daughters, Rachel and Julie . . .
who have helped me discover and relish numerous
Timely Insights Into Timeless Truth

Foreword

These are quick, but great. They get your attention, and then your heart.

I really like Ken's approach. The Timeless Truth for the day is introduced by a story about Madonna, or Walter Payton, or even some math teacher. You're there. You're interested.

And then you see how this is for you, and for today.

Yes! Adrenaline for the heart and spirit!

Knute Larson
Pastor, The Chapel, Akron, Ohio

A Timely Insight into . . .

Steve Camp, a contemporary Christian musician, said he went to a Motley Crue concert a decade ago to see why they drew such large crowds. He discovered,

"They are more sold out to their sin than we are to Jesus Christ."

What a dramatic wake-up call for the twenty-first century church!

Here is an equally vivid wake-up call from the first-century church:

Timeless Truth

Awake to righteousness, and sin not;
for some have not the knowledge of God:
I speak this to your shame.

1 Corinthians 15:34 (KJV)

A Timely Insight into . . .

A pastor concluded one Sunday morning service by instructing his people, "I would like all of you to read the 17th chapter of Mark's Gospel before next Sunday." The following Sunday, true to his word, he asked the congregation, "How many of you actually read the 17th chapter of Mark's Gospel this past week?" Almost everyone in the congregation raised their hands to signify that they had read it.

The pastor stunned his people by announcing,

"Ladies and gentlemen, there is no 17th chapter of Mark."

Then he launched into his Sunday morning sermon, which just happened to be about lying.

Timeless Truth

The Lord detests lying lips, but he delights in men who are truthful.

Proverbs 12:22

2

A Timely Insight into . . .

I once heard Cody Risien of the Cleveland Browns share a testimony of how God has worked in his life. He summed up his days as a young Christian playing football in the National Football League this way:

"God was in my life, but He wasn't all my life."

A year later I heard motivational guru Zig Ziglar offer this tip for young Christians like Cody Risien who are struggling in their walk with God:

> "I don't worship a part-time Lord,
> so I don't serve him on a part-time basis."

Timeless Truth

"Not everyone who says to Me, 'Lord, Lord,' will enter the kingdom of heaven, but only he who does the will of My Father who is in heaven."

Matthew 7:21

A Timely Insight into . . .

After I graduated from seminary, our family moved to Ashland, Ohio, so that I could serve in a pastoral internship program. We rented a house for that year. When the internship was completed, I accepted a call to become the pastor of a church in Akron, Ohio. But before our family could move into the house we bought in Akron, we lived in the church for a couple of weeks. The congregation was very small, and no other arrangements were possible.

When we finally did take possession of our house—our very first house—we went over late in the afternoon to move in a few things so we could stay in our new home that night. Then we decided to hit McDonald's. As we backed into the street our daughter Rachel, who was almost three, looked back up toward the house and asked,

"Are we all done living at that house now?"

Timeless Truth

All these people were still living by faith when they died. . . .
And they admitted that they were aliens
and strangers on earth.

Hebrews 11:13

A Timely Insight into . . .

A clever Jewish proverb, old enough to have whiskers, suggests:

"If the rich could hire people to die for them, the poor could make a wonderful living."

Forrest Gump, that whimsical post modern philosopher, insisted on his mama's old adage instead. "Life is like a box of chocolates," he mused. I hate to have to disagree with the all-wise Gump, but life is much more like a chess game. In chess, when you have finished playing, all of the pieces end up in the same box. Likewise, when life is over, the bishops, knights, kings, and queens all go into a box, along with all the pawns.

Timeless Truth

For the wise man, like the fool, will not be long remembered;
in days to come, both will be forgotten.
Like the fool, the wise man too must die!

Ecclesiastes 2:16

A Timely Insight into . . .

Everyone knows someone who has cheated on a test. But some recent surveys suggest that today's students have elevated cheating to an art form. It has become a national epidemic. Madison Sarratt, a math professor at Vanderbilt University, offered a sure-fire cure for cheating many years ago. He would instruct the students in his trigonometry class:

"Today I am giving two examinations, one in trigonometry and the other in honesty. I hope you will pass them both. If you must fail one, fail trigonometry. There are many good people in the world who can't pass trigonometry, but there are no good people who cannot pass the examination of honesty."

Isn't it nice to know that you can still be a good person, even if you don't understand (or even appreciate) trigonometry?

Timeless Truth

An honest answer is like a kiss on the lips.

Proverbs 24:26

A Timely Insight into . . .

Everyone who loves to read, dreams of writing a book. For most of us, it is probably just a pipe-dream. For those who succeed in publishing a book, it might seem more like a nightmare. Writing is a love-hate relationship. "It is a bloody art," the British would say.

But one frustrated American author testified,
> "Writing is easy; all you do is sit staring at a blank sheet of paper until the drops of blood form on your forehead."

Another teased,
> **"There's nothing to writing.
> All you do is sit down at a typewriter and open a vein."**

Not exactly a locker room pep talk for aspiring authors, is it?

Another author resorted to trash-talking to describe his craft:
> "The wastebasket is a writer's best friend."

Another quipped:
> "I love being a writer, What I can't stand is the paperwork."

Maybe Solomon was right, after all!

Timeless Truth

*Be warned, my son . . . Of making many books there is no end,
and much study wearies the body.*

Ecclesiastes 12:12

A Timely Insight into . . .

Some would say,

>"Faith is believing in spite of the evidence to the contrary."

Or worse yet, others would argue:

>"Faith is believing in spite of the fact that there is nothing to believe."

And one little guy in Sunday School defined faith this way:

>**"Faith is believing something you know isn't true."**

How many people, do you suppose, would agree with him? Too many? Would you? Or do you prefer this rock-ribbed definition?

Timeless Truth

>*Now faith is being sure of what we hope*
>*for and certain of what we do not see.*

Hebrews 11:1

A Timely Insight into . . .

Do you remember Sonny Jurgenson, the quarterback of the Washington Redskins? At one point during his career, he was taking his lumps from the fans and sportswriters alike because the Redskins were in a slump. Somebody asked him if all the carping was getting to him. He flashed a big grin and replied,

"Naw, not me. I've been in this game long enough to know that every week the quarterback is either in the penthouse or the outhouse!"

Everyone has to live with critics. Even the best of us!

Timeless Truth

For John the Baptist came neither eating bread nor drinking wine, and you say, "He has a demon." The Son of Man came eating and drinking, and you say, "Here is a glutton and a drunkard, a friend of tax collectors and sinners."

Luke 7:33–34

A Timely Insight into . . .

Walter Payton ran only nine miles during his entire career as the star running back of the Chicago Bears.

It doesn't sound too impressive when you look at it that way, does it? But what you need to remember is that he ran those nine miles, a grand total of 15,800 yards, while getting knocked down every 4.6 yards. Every five yards meant one more punishing tackle. That's why Payton was a shoo-in to the Pro Football Hall of Fame.

Nobody will care how many times you are knocked down in life . . . as long as you keep getting back up on your feet.

Timeless Truth

Everyone who competes in the games goes into strict training. They do it to get a crown that will not last; but we do it to get a crown that will last forever.

1 Corinthians 9:25

A Timely Insight into . . .

After an auto accident I took my car for repairs to a body shop in Columbus, Ohio. (Yes, the accident was my fault! Thanks for asking!) At the body shop I saw these words on a wood carving:

Today is the tomorrow we worried about yesterday, and all is well.

What do you get for all of your worries? (Besides an ulcer, I mean). Is it really necessary to borrow tomorrow's potential problems when there are more than enough real problems to keep you hopping today?

Timeless Truth

Therefore do not worry about tomorrow, for tomorrow will worry about itself. Each day has enough trouble of its own.

Matthew 6:34

A Timely Insight into . . .

Jackie Mason, the comedian, joked:

**"Money is not the most important thing in the world.
Love is. Fortunately, I love money."**

Ouch! Does that hit a bit too close to home for you, too?

The Bible teaches that "the love of money is the root of all evil." Not money. The love of money!

In other words, you don't have to have a Swiss bank account. You may only wish with all your might that you had one. The danger is just as real.

Timeless Truth

No one can serve two masters. Either he will hate the one and love the other, or he will be devoted to the one and despise the other. You cannot serve both God and Money.

Matthew 6:24

A Timely Insight into . . .

The evangelist, D.L. Moody, was convinced that the Bible was relevant to everyone, regardless of position or personality. He prescribed:

If you are impatient, sit down quietly and commune with Job.

If you are strong headed, read of Moses and Peter.

If you are weak-kneed, look at Elijah.

If there is no song in your heart, listen to David.

If you are a politician, read Daniel.

If you are getting sordid, read Isaiah.

If you are chilly, read of the beloved disciple.

If your faith is low, read Paul.

If you are getting lazy, watch James.

If you are losing sight of the future,
    read in Revelation of the promised land.

Timeless Truth

Open my eyes that I may see wonderful things in your law.

Psalm 119:18

A Timely Insight into . . .

Caution: the words you are about to read will jolt you. Be forewarned: these are not the sentiments of a liberal scholar involved in the Jesus Seminar. These forceful words were spit from the pen of Donald Grey Barnhouse, an "old-time religion" Presbyterian. At first glance, it may sound like Barnhouse was skeptical about the resurrection of Jesus. Hardly! Instead, he was expressing his supreme confidence in the reality of the resurrection.

> **"But if Jesus Christ is a man and only a man, then I say let us put Him among the execrated of history. If He is not risen, let us find the tomb that houses His dead body, let us give His bones to the dogs and expose Him to all the vilification that was heaped upon the body of a Mussolini."**

His point? Don't pay lip-service to Jesus as a great moral teacher if you don't profess Him as the Living Lord. If He is not the latter, he is neither.

Are you aware of what the Italians did to Mussolini, the fascist dictator of Italy during the Second World War? The bodies of this fascist bully and his mistress were riddled with bullets and then strung up by the ankles in a public square. While reporters watched in astonishment, the indignities began. One man landed a savage kick to the Duce's head. A woman who had lost five sons in the war fired five bullets into his dead body, one for each son. Men and women urinated on his face to add greater insult. With loud screams and curses the Italians trampled the corpses.

This is the kind of indignity Barnhouse wished upon the bones of Jesus, if His claims were not true. If Jesus Christ did not rise from the dead, then none of His claims can be trusted. If He did rise from the dead, He is absolutely trustworthy.

Timeless Truth

And if Christ has not been raised, our preaching is useless and so is your faith. . . . And if Christ has not been raised, your faith is futile; you are still in your sins.

1 Corinthians 15:14 & 17

A Timely Insight into . . .

Salvation is not free!

Wait! Don't rip out this page. This is not heresy! It is absolutely true. Salvation is not free! It is a free gift . . . to us. But it cost God dearly!

You and I did not have two spiritual pennies to rub together. We were completely bankrupt. Penniless in God's eternal economy! If God had put any price-tag on His gift of salvation, it would have been out of our reach. He had to make it available to us as a gift, absolutely free! But Jesus paid a dear price to purchase that gift. Yet God, in His grace, never told us how much this great gift cost Him! If He had, our five trillion dollar National Debt would seem like a drop in the bucket.

Timeless Truth

You are not your own; you were bought at a price.

1 Corinthians 6:19–20

A Timely Insight into . . .

Romans 3:23 is one of the greatest statements of grace in the Bible.

"Wait a minute," you might be tempted to object. "How can you call that a great statement of grace? Isn't that the verse that indicts all of us as guilty of sin?"

Yes, indeed. But the answer to your objection is quite simple.

It doesn't tell us how far short we come!

Timeless Truth

. . . for all have sinned and fall short of the glory of God.

Romans 3:23

A Timely Insight into . . .

George Bernard Shaw, the Irish playwright and amateur philosopher, signed off from this life with a startling verdict. This was his dismal confession in Too True to Be Good:

"The science to which I pinned my faith is bankrupt. . . . Its counsels, which should have established the millennium, led instead directly to the suicide of Europe. I believed them once. . . . In their name I helped to destroy the faith of millions of worshippers in the temples of a thousand creeds. And now they look at me and witness the great tragedy of an atheist who has lost his faith."

**The saddest thing from birth to sod
Is a dying man who has no God.**

Timeless Truth

The fool says in his heart, "There is no God."

Psalm 14:1

A Timely Insight into . . .

Madonna, the rock star, was asked how she felt about posing in Playboy and Penthouse. She commented:

"I have never done anything I am ashamed of."

Now, that is a shame!

People like Madonna worship their glands and boast about doing what they should be ashamed of doing. They are turning cartwheels on the interstate to hell. Does knowing this make you angry, or does it break your heart?

Timeless Truth

*For, as I have often told you before and
now say again even with tears, many live as enemies
of the cross of Christ. Their destiny is destruction,
their god is their stomach, and their glory is in their
shame. Their mind is on earthly things.*

Philippians 3:18–19

A Timely Insight into . . .

One afternoon over lunch a man confessed to me that he had a persistent problem with hard-core pornography. He was not a new Christian. He had been a member of several good churches through the years. But he had succumbed to the temptation to frequent adult bookstores. He stunned me when he suggested,

"I think pornography is more addicting than crack."

However, pornography, unlike crack, is legal! (Don't confuse the issues of morality and legality.) The Great Physician prescribed a severe remedy for people who struggle with pornography and lust. No, not amputation! His point? Pay any price you must to get rid of sin in your life!

Timeless Truth

If your right eye causes you to sin, gouge it out and throw it away. . . . And if your right hand causes you to sin, cut it off and throw it away. It is better for you to lose one part of your body than for your whole body to go into hell.

Matthew 5:29–30

A Timely Insight into . . .

Does God predestine people to eternal life, or do people make a decision of their own free will without any interference from God? Are Christians eternally secure, or can they lose their salvation? Questions like these can start theological fist-fights.

John Calvin once remarked that no theologian is ever more than 80 percent correct.

Isn't that humbling? As your knowledge grows, the Bible says, pride tends to inflate like a balloon. Insert a biblical humility pin, and POP! Love is different. Love doesn't puff up. It builds up, on a solid foundation. If only people who wrestle with great theological questions would exercise more love and less logic.

Timeless Truth

We know that we all possess knowledge.
Knowledge puffs up, but love builds up.

1 Corinthians 8:1

A Timely Insight into . . .

We had some dinner guests after church one Sunday. We enjoyed a great meal and some enthusiastic dinner conversation. But our daughter Julie, who was five at the time, was the real highlight of the afternoon.

She reached for her glass of milk, but couldn't quite get her hands on it. One of our dinner guests noticed her plight. "Here, I'll get it for you, Julie," he offered. But Julie refused his help. Instead she announced,

"I can reach it with my knees."

Which she did! Kneeling in her chair, Julie reached out and grabbed her glass of milk.

There are many things in this life that we can reach only with our knees.

Timeless Truth

You want something but don't get it. You kill and covet,
but you cannot have what you want. You quarrel and fight.
You do not have, because you do not ask God.

James 4:2

A Timely Insight into . . .

Henry Heinz, the "ketchup king," left this unique testimonial in his will:

"Looking forward to the time when my earthly career will end, I desire to set forth at the very beginning of this will, as the most important item in it, a confession of my faith in Jesus Christ as my Savior. I also desire to bear witness to the fact that throughout my life, in which there were unusual joys and sorrows, I have been wonderfully sustained by my faith in God through Jesus Christ. This legacy was left me by my consecrated mother, a woman of strong faith, and to it I attribute any success I have attained."

I'll never pick up a bottle of ketchup the same ever again. Will you?

Timeless Truth

Therefore, since we are surrounded by such a great cloud of witnesses, let us throw off everything that hinders and the sin that so easily entangles, and let us run with perseverance the race marked out for us.

Hebrews 12:1

A Timely Insight into . . .

Try these ratios on for size:

**The size of a human cell is to that of a person
as a person's size is to that of Rhode Island.**

**Likewise, a virus is to a person
as a person is to the earth.**

**An atom is to a person
as a person is to the earth's orbit around the sun.**

**Finally, a proton is to a person
as a person is to the distance to Alpha Centauri.**

Does that give you a fresh appreciation for the wonder that David felt when he gazed up into the night sky?

Timeless Truth

*When I consider your heavens, the work of your fingers,
the moon and the stars, which you have set in place,
what is man that you are mindful of him,
the son of man that you care for him?*

Psalm 8:3–4

A Timely Insight into . . .

When my daughter Julie was four years old she couldn't say "L's." She substituted a "Y" for every "L" she pronounced. One night, I remember her coming over to me and asking, "Dad, can I climb up on your yap?"

In fun I teased, "Julie, that's not my yap" (pointing to my lap). "This is my yap" (pointing to my mouth).

"That's not your yap," she protested. "That's your yips."

Ah, yes! Those infamous "yips," as in "Read my yips." They often get us in trouble, don't they? Perhaps more than we realize!!!

Timeless Truth

"But I tell you that men will have to give account on the day of judgment for every careless word they have spoken."

Matthew 12:36

A Timely Insight into . . .

Syndicated columnist Bob Greene selected two men as the most influential Americans in the latter half of the 20th century. Who do you think made the list? Would you guess Billy Graham? Not even close. Even though year after year Graham's name can be found high on the list of people whom Americans respect.

Out of all possible occupations and professions, Greene identified Elvis Presley and Hugh Hefner as the greatest change-agents of the last half of the twentieth century. You may not like his picks, but you have to accept his logic:

"My point is that the world is very, very different from what it was 30 years ago. And the two people who symbolize that difference are Presley and Hefner. They literally have changed our lives, in ways that all others who have lived during these years could not have."

Is he right? Is that really true? Do you buy that? Can it be? Before you make up your mind about that, there is more. As bad as that analysis was, it gets worse. Greene's assessment of the character of these two men was the icing on the cake.

"It is rapidly becoming apparent that Presley, in his private life, was something of a pathetic goofball; and Hefner . . . is a classic weirdo."

Isn't that a dreadful commentary on American life in the last half of the twentieth century? A "classic weirdo" and a "pathetic goofball" have exerted more influence over the lives of ordinary Americans than any other public figures in the last fifty years. Including Billy Graham! Is that a fair assessment? Well . . . consider this: Have we climbed toward the moral high ground in recent decades, or have we been sinking into a moral swamp? Enough said?

Timeless Truth

"This is your lot, the portion I have decreed for you,"
declares the LORD, "because you have forgotten me and
trusted in false gods. I will pull up your skirts over
your face that your shame may be seen . . . "

Jeremiah 13:25–26

A Timely Insight into . . .

Charles Darwin, in his Descent of Man, predicted:

"At some future period, the civilized races of man will almost certainly exterminate and replace the savage races throughout the world."

Thomas Huxley, Darwin's bulldog, bared his fangs against blacks in 1901:

"No rational man, cognizant of the facts, believes that the average Negro is the equal, still less the superior of the average white man."

These are the theorists that inspired Herbert Spencer's famous dictum: "the survival of the fittest." Today, we call this racism, not science!

Timeless Truth

*They exchanged the truth of God for a lie,
and worshiped and served created things rather than the
Creator—who is forever praised. Amen.*

Romans 1:25

A Timely Insight into . . .

Margaret Sanger, the founder of Planned Parenthood, coined the slogan:

"More children from the fit, less from the unfit."

Where do you think she drew her inspiration for that slogan? If you guessed Charles Darwin, you guessed right. But it gets worse. She described blacks and European immigrants as "human weeds." Then Sanger developed "the Negro Project," about which she warned an associate:

"We do not want word to get out that we want to exterminate the Negro population."

I wonder what else Planned Parenthood has planned!

Timeless Truth

For although they knew God, they neither glorified him as God nor gave thanks to him, but their thinking became futile and their foolish hearts were darkened.

Romans 1:21

A Timely Insight into . . .

Margaret Sanger's father fancied himself a freethinker and a skeptic. One day while Margaret was a little girl, she was reciting the Lord's Prayer. When she came to the phrase, "Give us this day our daily bread," her father interrupted.

"Who were you talking to?" he asked.

"To God," she replied.

"Well tell me, is God a baker?"

"No, of course not," she gulped. "But he makes the rain, the sunshine, and all the things that make the wheat, which makes the bread."

"Well, well, so that's the idea," her father chided. "Then why didn't you just say so? Always say what you mean, my daughter; it is much better."

Unfortunately, Margaret's cynical father succeeded in turning her heart away from her heavenly Father. Many other children, guilty only of the crime of being unborn, have paid for his treachery with their very lives.

Timeless Truth

Fathers, do not exasperate your children; instead,
bring them up in the training and instruction of the Lord.

Ephesians 6:4

A Timely Insight into . . .

Martin Luther once remarked:

"If God had all the answers in his right hand, and the struggle to reach those answers in his left, I would choose God's left hand."

Which hand would you choose?

Beware: your choice could tell more about you than you care to know. Do you understand what the Bible tells you about your struggles and troubles? Are you aware that God wants to use your suffering to make you better not bitter, and better fit for your *future*?

Timeless Truth

For our light and momentary troubles are achieving for us an eternal glory that far outweighs them all.

2 Corinthians 4:17

A Timely Insight into . . .

"If you were Noah and there was a flood today, and you could pick out the people to live with you on the ark to start the world over again, whom would you choose?"

That question was directed to George Bernard Shaw, the great playwright. His cynical reply was,

"I'd let them all drown!"

Aren't you glad that Mr. Shaw was not appointed to be the savior of the world? What if Jesus had adopted that approach?

Timeless Truth

Here is a trustworthy saying that deserves full acceptance:
Christ Jesus came into the world
to save sinners—of whom I am the worst.

1 Timothy 1:15

A Timely Insight into . . .

Mark Russell quipped:

"Recent surveys suggest that most people who favor abortion have already been born!"

Have you heard the latest abortion rights rhetoric? Pro-life advocates have now been labeled "anti-choice." It is the latest attempt to intimidate abortion opponents. I heard a great come-back to this new moniker recently. A pro-life advocate described pro-abortion advocates as "**anti-life**." Which would you rather be: Anti-choice or anti-life? It's an easy choice, don't you think?

Timeless Truth

For you created my inmost being; you knit me together in my mother's womb. I praise you because I am fearfully and wonderfully made . . . My frame was not hidden from you when I was made in the secret place. When I was woven together in the depths of the earth, your eyes saw my unformed body. All the days ordained for me were written in your book before one of them came to be.

Psalm 139:13–16

A Timely Insight into . . .

Someone said, "The golden rule of matrimony is `You shall love your wife as yourself.'"

Winston Churchill once attended a formal banquet in London. A number of dignitaries and celebrities were present. The question was asked, "If you could not be who you are, who would you like to be?"

Everyone present took a turn answering the question. When it was Churchill's turn, the old man stood to his feet and gave a classic answer.

"If I could not be who I am, I would most like to be Lady Churchill's second husband."

"Good show, Winston!" The old boy made some points that night.

Timeless Truth

In this same way, husbands ought to love their wives
as their own bodies. He who loves his wife loves himself.

Ephesians 5:28

A Timely Insight into . . .

During the battle of Bull Run, Confederate General Stonewall Jackson received a painful wound. One of his fellow officers asked him, "General, how is it that you can keep so cool and appear so utterly insensible to danger, in such a storm of shell and bullets as rained about you when your hand was hit?"

"Captain," answered Jackson, in a grave and reverential manner, "**my religious belief teaches me to feel as safe in battle as in bed.** God has fixed the time for my death. I do not concern myself about that, but to be always ready, no matter when it may overtake me." After a pregnant pause he added, "That is the way all men should live, and then all the world would be brave."

Timeless Truth

I eagerly expect and hope that I will in no way
be ashamed, but will have sufficient courage so that
now as always Christ will be exalted in my body,
whether by life or by death.

Philippians 1:20

A Timely Insight into . . .

Dr. Duong Quynh Hoa joined the Communist party while she was in medical school in Paris in the early 1950's. After her return to Vietnam, she served as a covert Vietnamese agent while she practiced medicine in Saigon. She often hid in the jungles and traveled abroad on propaganda missions for the NVA. Later, she was appointed as the Deputy Minister of Health in the "provisional revolutionary government" of the Vietcong. One evening in 1981, in her comfortable villa decorated with exquisite Chinese and Vietnamese porcelains, she confessed her disappointment with Communism to an American journalist:

"I've been a Communist all my life. But now, for the first time, I have seen the realities of Communism. It is failure, mismanagement, corruption, privilege, repression. My ideals are gone."

Timeless Truth

Remember your Creator in the days of your youth,
before the days of trouble come and the years approach
when you will say, "I find no pleasure in them."

Ecclesiastes 12:1

A Timely Insight into . . .

Our 36th President, Lyndon Johnson, used to love to tell this story on himself. When he ran for the Senate in Texas for the first time, he gathered a group of friends one night and led them all into a cemetery. They copied the names off the tombstones so that they could enter them on the voting rolls. On election night, they would be counted along with those who voted for Johnson.

As they maneuvered among the rows of tombstones they came to an old marker overgrown with moss. It was difficult to read. One of the volunteers said to Johnson, "This one is hard to read. I'm going to skip it." Johnson disagreed.

"You will not skip it. He's got as much right to vote as anybody in this cemetery."

Timeless Truth

Do not lie to each other, since you have taken off your old self with its practices . . .

Colossians 3:9

A Timely Insight into . . .

Sparky Anderson, the manager of baseball's Detroit Tigers, made a candid admission in 1984. It was the year that the Tigers swept through the regular season, the playoffs, and the World Series without any serious opposition. This gem actually appeared in the Detroit News:

> "But I'm not lying when I say that this (religion) is so important to me. If I had one great wish, it would be that I could honestly say that I was one of His [God's] people. That's the one emptiness I have.

> **"I'd give up all the pennants and all the honors just to know that I was doing right by Him."**

Timeless Truth

Again, the kingdom of heaven is like a merchant looking for fine pearls. When he found one of great value, he went away and sold everything he had and bought it.

Matthew 13:45–46

38

A Timely Insight into . . .

H. Richard Neibuhr indicted liberal theologians for preaching

> "a God without wrath [bringing] men without sin into a kingdom without judgment through the ministrations of a Christ without a cross."

Those are the terms that many people today have dictated to God. "I will accept you on those terms, or not at all," they insist.

I have news for you. God will not accept your terms. He will accept only your full and unconditional surrender.

Religion without repentance is repugnant to God.

Timeless Truth

. . . having a form of godliness but denying its power.
Have nothing to do with them.

2 Timothy 3:5

A Timely Insight into . . .

Some clever fellow wrote this catchy bit of verse:

He held me close—
    a chill ran down my spine.
I thought it was love,
    but it was just his Popsicle melting.

Too many people get married because they're "in love."
Unfortunately, that doesn't mean that they are in love with another
person. It simply means that they are in love with the feeling
of being "in love." Love is much more than a fuzzy feeling or a
sentimental emotion.

Timeless Truth

Love is patient, love is kind. It does not envy, it does not boast,
it is not proud. It is not rude, it is not self-seeking, it is not
easily angered, it keeps no record of wrongs. Love does not
delight in evil but rejoices with the truth. It always protects,
always trusts, always hopes, always perseveres. Love never fails.

1 Corinthians 13:4–8

A Timely Insight into . . .

Dick Halverson, a retired pastor and recent Chaplain of the U.S. Senate, observed:

> "In the beginning the church was a fellowship of men and women centering on the living Christ. . . .
>
> Then the church moved to Greece where it became a **philosophy**. Then it moved to Rome where it became an **institution**. Next, it moved to Europe where it became a **culture**. And, finally, it moved to America where it became an **enterprise**."

When Jesus said, "I will build My church, and the gates of Hades will not overcome it," do you think that is what He had in mind? Or did He envision something far greater and much grander?

Timeless Truth

. . . God's household, which is the church of the living God, the pillar and foundation of the truth.

1 Timothy 3:15

41

A Timely Insight into . . .

Like so many little guys did in those days, I used to trade baseball cards. "I'll trade you these three cards for your Willie Mays or Mickey Mantle," was an offer that might be refused. For good reason. But Gerald Mann's deal is too good to pass up, even for an experienced trader like me:

To trade my "if onlys" for "next times"
>is to let go of my past and leave it to God.

To trade my "what-ifs" for "so whats"
>is to give my future to God.

To knock the T out of my "can'ts"
>is to give today to God.

Timeless Truth

Brothers, I do not consider myself yet to have taken hold of it. But one thing I do: Forgetting what is behind and straining toward what is ahead, I press on toward the goal to win the prize for which God has called me heavenward in Christ Jesus.

Philippians 3:13–14

A Timely Insight into . . .

Madison Avenue hawks pizzas by asking, "What do you want on your tombstone?" Some strange and wonderful things have found their way onto grave stones. Like this epitaph for an old maid in Scranton, PA:

No hits,
No runs,
No heirs.

But Charles Spurgeon advised,

"A good character is the best tombstone. Those who loved you and were helped by you will remember you when forget-me-nots are withered. Carve your name on hearts, and not on marble."

Timeless Truth

The righteous man leads a blameless life;
blessed are his children after him.

Proverbs 20:7

43

A Timely Insight into . . .

"Football combines the two worst things about American life. It is violence punctuated by committee meetings."

Maybe George Will was right. I had never thought of equating huddles with committee meetings, but there is an uncanny resemblance.

Few people would actually admit that they love doing committee work. But everybody would agree with a friend of mine who loved to remind us all:

"For God so loved the world that He didn't send a committee."

Timeless Truth

For God so loved the world that he gave his one and only Son, that whoever believes in him shall not perish but have eternal life.

John 3:16

A Timely Insight into . . .

Sharon Begley gave this rather technical description of the theoretical "Big Bang" in Newsweek:

" . . . after the big bang 12 billion years ago, the infant universe inflated wildly to some 10 trillion times its original size in about a sextillionth of a pico second."

What in the world is a "pico second"?

And who really cares? Besides, how does she know what happened at ground zero of the universe? Was she there? God was!

Timeless Truth

"Where were you when I laid the earth's foundation? Tell me, if you understand. Who marked off its dimensions? Surely you know! Who stretched a measuring line across it?"

Job 38:4–5

A Timely Insight into . . .

Imagine this scene: You are standing on the seashore. A ship in the harbor spreads her white sails to the morning breeze and starts for the blue ocean. She is an object of beauty and strength, and you stand and watch her until at length she hangs like a speck of white cloud just where the sea rises and the sky comes down to meet each other. Then someone at your side observes,

"There, she is gone."

Gone where? Gone from your sight, that is all. She is just as large in mast and hull and spar as she was when she left the harbor, and just as able to bear her load of living weights to its place of destination. Her diminished size is in you, not in her; and just at the moment when someone at your side says, "There, she is gone," on that distant shore there are other eyes watching for her coming and other voices ready to take up the glad shout,

"Here she comes!"

Timeless Truth

We are confident, I say, and would prefer
to be away from the body and at home with the Lord.

2 Corinthians 5:8

A Timely Insight into . . .

There are always voices prepared to sound the alarm about dark, foreboding skies looming on the economic horizon. In the early 1990s one author bemoaned, The Coming Economic Earthquake, and a different author celebrated, The Great Boom Ahead. Who was right? Maybe we should pay more attention to the person who noted, "If all economists were laid end to end, they'd point in all directions."

I do know that this clever soul had a point when he delineated three distinct stages of economic woe:

Recession: When the man next door loses his job.
Depression: When you lose your job.
Panic: When your wife loses her job.

Whatever happened to caring for others and bearing one another's burdens?

Timeless Truth

Carry each other's burdens,
and in this way you will fulfill the law of Christ.

Galatians 6:2

A Timely Insight into . . .

You may never have seen this notice posted in the office of an accounting firm:

"In God we trust, all others we audit."

But you've probably seen this little sign posted someplace:

"In God we trust, all others pay cash."

But here is one that is guaranteed to make you smile. It was seen in a restaurant in Fort Lauderdale, Florida.

IF YOU ARE OVER 80 YEARS OLD
AND ACCOMPANIED BY YOUR PARENTS
WE WILL CASH YOUR CHECK

Timeless Truth

The man of integrity walks securely,
but he who takes crooked paths will be found out.

Proverbs 10:9

David Garrick, the actor, conducted a private tour of Hampton Court for his friend, Dr. Samuel Johnson. As they walked through the stately mansion with its lovely paintings, and the picturesque gardens with their impressive statues, Dr. Johnson remarked,

"Ah, David, David, these are the things which make a deathbed terrible."

We all know this to be true, but we forget it almost as often. This same Dr. Johnson, the English "man of letters," drilled this home:

"People need to be reminded more often than they need to be instructed."

Don't forget: You will never see a hearse pulling a U-haul trailer.

Timeless Truth

For we have brought nothing into the world,
so we cannot take anything out of it either.

1 Timothy 6:7 (NASB)

A Timely Insight into . . .

G. K. Chesterton is often quoted, but few know why. Many of his one-liners appear in print. He once described the United States as "a nation with the soul of a church." Alistair Cooke agreed. But, then, with a twist of the blade, he jabbed:

"That's true, but it also has the soul of a whorehouse."

Does that offend you? Is that outrageous?

Well, is it? Can you argue with his logic when the covers of videos and magazines ooze sex, and the deep, dark recesses of the Internet are amply stocked with every kind of pornography imaginable?

Timeless Truth

Then the LORD said to me in the days of Josiah the king,
"Have you seen what faithless Israel did?
She went up on every high hill and under every
green tree, and she was a harlot there."

Jeremiah 3:6 (NASB)

A Timely Insight into . . .

Out with that "worm theology," we moderns and post moderns demand. We can't imagine why a man would ask to have these words engraved on his tombstone:

> William Carey
> Born August 17th, 1761
> Died June 1834
> A wretched, poor and helpless worm,
> on Thy kind arms I fall.

Today, we would say, "My, he had low self-esteem."

Wrong!

He was a gutsy pioneer, the Father of modern missions. His "double-dog dare" still echoes off the canyon walls of time:

> "Attempt great things for God.
> Expect great things from God."

If that is low self-esteem, . . . May his tribe increase!

Timeless Truth

For with God nothing will be impossible.

Luke 1:37 (NKJV)

A Timely Insight into . . .

A senator addressed his fellow lawmakers with this stunning analysis of a national crisis:

"I fear for our nation. Nearly half of our people receive some form of government subsidy. We have grown weak from too much affluence and too little adversity. I fear that soon we will not be able to defend our country from our sure and certain enemies. We have debased our currency to the point that even the most loyal citizen no longer trusts it."

Which of our U.S. senators do you suppose had the courage to speak his mind so freely? The answer is . . . none of the above. These words were spoken by a Roman senator in AD 63.

Timeless Truth

That which has been is that which will be, And that which has been done is that which will be done. So, there is nothing new under the sun.

Ecclesiastes 1:9 (NASB)

A Timely Insight into . . .

When he died, his empire was *four* times the size of Alexander's and more than *twice* the size of the Roman empire. But it survived less than 200 hundred years. Who was this world-class conqueror? None other than Genghis Khan, the ambitious leader of the Mongol hordes. On his deathbed the Great Khan was wrapped in blankets, shivering before a small fire. He was delirious with pain, and complained:

"My descendants will wear gold, they will eat the choicest meats, they will ride the finest horses, they will hold in their arms the most beautiful women and they will forget to whom they owe it all."

Timeless Truth

. . . and when your herds and your flocks multiply, and your silver and gold multiply, and all that you have multiplies, then your heart will become proud and you will forget the LORD *your God who brought you out from the land of Egypt, out of the house of slavery.*

Deuteronomy 8:13–14

A Timely Insight into . . .

I will never forget what Harold Sala told a group of pastors in Akron, Ohio. He deposited into our ministry kits three simple truths. But I would score his third point with a squirm-factor of 10!

1. Every person needs the Savior
2. Every person is worth saving—they are worth reaching
3. *Their salvation is more important than your personal comfort.*

When the meeting ended, I introduced myself to him and told him how convicting his third point was to me. I told him that I had never heard anybody say anything like that. I was stunned when he responded,

"Ken, we really don't believe there's a hell."

Timeless Truth

*It is a dreadful thing to fall into the hands
of the living God.*

Hebrews 10:31

A Timely Insight into . . .

More than eighty million people in the United States claim to have no church affiliation at all. Another ninety million are affiliated with a church but are not actively attending one. Only six other nations in the world have a total population larger than eighty million.

Years ago several pastors were discussing the challenge of world missions with a veteran African missionary. They asked him, "What is the greatest mission field in the entire world today?" He did not hesitate as he responded,

"Without any question, it is the great American city."

Timeless Truth

How deserted lies the city, once so full of people! How like a widow is she, who once was great among the nations! She who was queen among the provinces has now become a slave.

Lamentations 1:1

A Timely Insight into . . .

Chiang Kai Shek was the leader of the Nationalist Chinese government in exile on Taiwan until his death in 1975. He failed in his attempt to oppose Mao Tse Tung, the leader of the Communist Chinese, and was forced to evacuate from Mainland China. He was largely forgotten about by the U.S. after President Nixon made his infamous trips to Red China. But perhaps this testimony from his own lips will make you think twice about him:

"The most important thing about my life is 'I was a follower of Jesus Christ.'"

I think that is the most important thing that can be said about anyone's life!

Timeless Truth

For we do not preach ourselves but Christ Jesus as Lord,
and ourselves as your bond-servants for Jesus' sake.

2 Corinthians 4:5 (NASB)

A Timely Insight into . . .

Bruce Catton, editor of American Heritage and a leading authority on the Civil War, gave a speech on the theme "What 1861 Has to Say to 1961." He dedicated three-quarters of his remarks to a contrast of weaponry and the science of war between 1861 and 1961. The rest of his talk was addressed to what he declared to be history's greatest problem; namely, human nature, the most explosive fact in history. He finished his lecture by pointing out that the problem of 1961 is identical to that of 1861. In fact, he argued that the problem was as old as time immemorial.

"The problem in 1961 AD is identical to that of 1961 BC; it is man himself."

Timeless Truth

The heart is deceitful above all things and beyond cure. Who can understand it?

Jeremiah 17:9

A Timely Insight into . . .

After graduation from high school, William Borden's father sent young William on a cruise around the world. He was brokenhearted by the spiritual needs of the people he met. Therefore he committed his life to serve the Lord Jesus Christ as a missionary. He wrote in his journal:

> "Say 'no' to self, 'yes' to Jesus every time. . . . In every man's heart there is a throne and a cross. If Christ is on the throne, self is on the cross; and if self, even a little bit, is on the throne, Jesus is on the cross in that man's heart . . . Lord, I take my hands off, as far as my life is concerned. I put Thee on the throne of my life. Change, cleanse, use me as Thou shalt choose."

He planned to go to China. But first he sailed to Egypt. There he contracted spinal meningitis and died within a month. Some people said, "What a waste." But when his will was probated, it was discovered that he had left his entire fortune of over $1 million to be invested in the cause of Christ. Three unforgettable phrases preserved in this young man's diary summarize his life:

No reserves . . . No retreat . . . No regrets

Timeless Truth

"If anyone comes to me and does not hate his father
and mother, his wife and children, his brothers and sisters—
yes, even his own life—he cannot be my disciple."

Luke 14:26

A Timely Insight into . . .

Billy Graham was party to an unusual conversation in Communist China. He was sitting beside a top Chinese Communist leader at a luncheon hosted by the American ambassador. Billy asked the Communist, "Why is Christianity growing so fast in China?" The man's response was astonishing:

"Persecution. If you want to evangelize China, just persecute Christians. The more they are persecuted, the faster the church grows."

Maybe the fellow who said, "Christians are like tea bags. They are no good until they're thrown in hot water," was on to something.

Timeless Truth

"Remember the words I spoke to you:
'No servant is greater than his master.'
If they persecuted me, they will persecute you also."

John 15:20

A Timely Insight into . . .

F.B. Meyer, the famous British preacher, once spent a night as a house guest in the home of A.B. Simpson, the founder of the Christian and Missionary Alliance. Early the next morning, Mr. Meyer stole quietly downstairs, thinking he was the first one up.

But no; there through the partially open door to the study, he could see A.B. Simpson in prayer. He had a world globe in front of him, and he would put his finger on a spot, and pray. Then he would spin it, put his finger on another spot, and pray.

Then, as F.B. Meyer watched . . .

A.B. Simpson leaned forward, wrapped his arms around the globe, hugged it, and cried.

Timeless Truth

When he saw the crowds, he had compassion on them, because they were harassed and helpless, like sheep without a shepherd.

Matthew 9:36

A Timely Insight into . . .

Carl Jung, Freud's ex-disciple, submitted himself to a film interview toward the end of his life. After a number of prosaic questions, the interviewer asked, "Dr. Jung, a lot of your writing has a religious flavor. Do you believe in God?"

Jung puffed on his pipe, and then mused out loud, "Believe in God? Well, we use the word 'believe' when we think that something is true but we don't yet have a substantial body of evidence to support it.

"No. I don't believe in God. I know there's a God!"

Timeless Truth

For since the creation of the world God's invisible qualities—his eternal power and divine nature—have been clearly seen, being understood from what has been made, so that men are without excuse.

Romans 1:20

A Timely Insight into . . .

Mother Teresa was the keynote speaker at the National Prayer Breakfast on February 3, 1994, in Washington D.C. The President and Mrs. Clinton, who are pro-choice, sat less than ten feet away from this 4' 6" titan. When she began to speak, she did not address either the president or vice-president. She ignored all protocol. Instead, she spoke from her heart and shot from the hip:

"But I feel that the greatest destroyer of peace today is abortion, because it is a war against the child, a direct killing of the innocent child, murder by the mother herself. And if we accept that a mother can kill even her own child, how can we tell other people not to kill one another?"

Timeless Truth

Before I formed you in the womb I knew you,
before you were born I set you apart;
I appointed you as a prophet to the nations.

Jeremiah 1:5

A Timely Insight into . . .

Many years ago two young women signed Hollywood movie contracts at the same time. They were determined to be great movie stars. A few years later, one of the young women, Colleen Townsend, became a Christian and married a Presbyterian minister. The other young woman lived the "dream" and became a sex symbol in Hollywood. She was married several times. Several years passed before these two women met one another. The other young woman, Marilyn Monroe, admitted to Colleen Townsend Evans,

"When I signed that contract I was determined to be a star, whatever it cost me, whatever I had to do. My dream has been fulfilled, but I have paid too much for what I have gotten. I am the most miserable and unhappy person in the world."

Timeless Truth

Yet when I surveyed all that my hands had done and what I had toiled to achieve, everything was meaningless, a chasing after the wind; nothing was gained under the sun.

Ecclesiastes 2:11

A Timely Insight into . . .

Matthew Henry's comments on the Bible are ageless. Written in the 18th century, they are often more relevant to the 21st century. There is a wonderful story about this godly man that has survived all these many years. He had been mugged and his money purse was stolen. Yet, when he reflected back on this miserable experience, this is what he recorded in his diary:

"Let me be thankful, first, because I was never robbed before; second, because, although they took my purse, they did not take my life; third, because, although they took my all, it was not much, and fourth, because it was I who was robbed, not I who robbed."

Now, that is gratitude for ya'!

Timeless Truth

Be joyful always; pray continually; give thanks in all circumstances, for this is God's will for you in Christ Jesus.

1 Thessalonians 5:16–18

A Timely Insight into . . .

Dawson Trotman, the founder of the Navigators, had an intriguing bed-time habit. When conversation had ended, and all the lights were out, he would announce, "H.W.L.W." Then someone would recite a passage of Scripture without making any other comment. **H.W.L.W. equals "His Word the Last Word."** It was a great way to end a day with one's thoughts fixed on the Word of God.

If we were to practice that, it would give a new meaning to bed-time reading, wouldn't it?

Timeless Truth

These commandments that I give you today are to be
upon your hearts. Impress them on your children.
Talk about them when you sit at home and when you walk
along the road, when you lie down and when you get up.

Deuteronomy 6:6–7

A Timely Insight into . . .

William Lyon Phelps (1865–1943), whose students for years voted him "Yale's most inspiring professor," said, without apology:

"I believe a knowledge of the Bible without a college course is more valuable than a college course without a Bible."

Jonathon Witherspoon, the first president of the College of New Jersey (renamed Princeton University) operated the school by this mandate:

"Cursed be all learning that is contrary to the cross of Christ."

"Cursed be all learning that is not coincident with the cross of Christ."

"Cursed be all learning that is not subservient to the cross of Christ."

We've come a long way, baby! But do you like where we are?

Timeless Truth

But mark this: There will be terrible times in the last days. . . .
always learning but never able to acknowledge the truth.

2 Timothy 3:1, 7

A Timely Insight into . . .

What was it that Art Linkletter used to say? "Kids Say the Darndest Things!" It is true of all kids. Even the great-great-grandkids of Presidents! William Howard Taft was the 27th President of the United States (1909–1913). His great-granddaughter, who was a third-grader in Cincinnati, Ohio, at the time, was asked to write a simple autobiography. Here was her life, abbreviated into one brief paragraph:

My name is Martha Bowers Taft. My great-grandfather was President of the United States of America. My grandfather was a United States senator. My daddy is ambassador to Ireland, and I am a Brownie.

Timeless Truth

Sons are a heritage from the LORD, children a reward from him. Like arrows in the hands of a warrior are sons born in one's youth. Blessed is the man whose quiver is full of them.

Psalm 127:3–5

A Timely Insight into . . .

Ernest Hemingway, in his short story, "The Capital of the World," tells about a father and his teenage son who lived in Spain. Their relationship became strained, eventually shattered, and the son ran away from home. The father began a long journey in search of the lost and rebellious son, finally putting an ad in the Madrid newspaper as a last resort. His son's name was Paco, a very common name in Spain.

The ad simply read:

Dear Paco,

Meet me in front of the Madrid newspaper office tomorrow at noon. All is forgiven. I love you.

The next day at noon there were 800 "Pacos" in front of the newspaper office, all seeking forgiveness.

Timeless Truth

Some men brought to him a paralytic, lying on a mat.
When Jesus saw their faith, he said to the paralytic,
"Take heart, son; your sins are forgiven."

Matthew 9:2

A Timely Insight into . . .

Helen Keller was asked one time, "What would be worse than being born blind?" She quickly replied,

"To have sight and no vision."

If you want to enhance your vision without looking through rose-colored glasses, try on this paraphrase of Ephesians 3:20. It is superb.

"You cannot out-ask me; you cannot out-think me; you cannot out-imagine me; you cannot out-dream me; you cannot out-do me; for I am able to do exceedingly abundantly above all that you ask or think."

Timeless Truth

Now to him who is able to do immeasurably more than all we ask or imagine, according to his power that is at work within us . . .

Ephesians 3:20

A Timely Insight into . . .

Rabindranath Tagore, the son of the Maharishi (or "Great Sage"), became a gifted composer and poet. He was awarded the Nobel Prize for Literature in 1913. He certainly knew whereof he spoke when he said,

I have on my table a violin string. It is free. I twist one end of it and it responds. It is free. But it is not free to do what a violin string is supposed to do—to produce music. So I take it, fix it in my violin, and tighten it until it is taut. Only then is it free to be a violin string.

Timeless Truth

Then you will know the truth, and the truth will set you free.

John 8:32

A Timely Insight into . . .

On baseball's opening day in 1954, the Cincinnati Reds played the Milwaukee Braves. Two rookies played their first major league game that afternoon.

Jim Greengrass, a rookie playing for the Reds, went 4 for 4 with four doubles! A rookie playing for the Braves that same day went 0 for 4. No hits!

You probably have never heard of the Red's rookie, Jim Greengrass. His career ended after just five mediocre seasons. However, I suspect that you will recognize the name of the Braves rookie who got off to such a dismal start. He played for twenty-three years, and became a baseball legend. His jersey, number 44, was retired by the Atlanta Braves after he smacked 755 home runs, 41 more than "the Babe." Did you already guess his name? I thought you would know the name, Hank Aaron.

Timeless Truth

Moreover, when God gives any man wealth and possessions,
and enables him to enjoy them, to accept his lot and
be happy in his work—this is a gift of God.

Ecclesiastes 5:19

A Timely Insight into . . .

Chuck Swindoll calls it "the law of echoes." Simply put, the law states: When you love, you will be loved. When you hate, you will be hated. So choose your own poison! Swindoll gave this example of this important spiritual law:

> I read recently about a teacher who asked a group of students to jot down, in 30 seconds, the names of the people they really disliked. Some of the students could think of only one person during that half minute. Others listed as many as 14.

The interesting fact that emerged from the research was—those who disliked the largest number of people were themselves the most widely disliked.

Timeless Truth

Do not judge, and you will not be judged. Do not condemn, and you will not be condemned. Forgive, and you will be forgiven.

Luke 6:37

A Timely Insight into . . .

Hugh Hefner, the Playboy king, who presumably can have all the sensual pleasure he wants, is reported to have said on one occasion,

"In the next ten years I would rather meet a girl and fall in love and have her fall in love with me than to make another 100 million dollars."

During the 1990s, Hef suffered a romantic breakdown. He got married! Perhaps what Mr. Playboy was really trying to say is this: "I've got it all, but I don't have satisfaction. There is something that is worth more than 100 million dollars to me, and I don't have it."

Timeless Truth

I thought in my heart, "Come now, I will test you with pleasure to find out what is good." But that also proved to be meaningless.

Ecclesiastes 2:1

A Timely Insight into . . .

John Flavel, a Puritan writer, drew this clever theological word picture:

**"The providence of God is like Hebrew words—
it can only be read backwards."**

Soren Kierkegaard, the Danish philosopher, erased the Puritan's theology, but painted an equally vivid picture with these words:

" . . . life can only be understood backwards,
but it must be lived forwards."

Today, we've reduced it further to this hip-hop proverb: Hindsight is always 20–20!

Timeless Truth

*Now these things occurred as examples to keep us
from setting our hearts on evil things as they did.*

1 Corinthians 10:6

A Timely Insight into . . .

One of those ancient Greek sages tried to drill some uncommon sense into the heads of "workaholics":

Could I climb the highest place in Athens, I would lift my voice and proclaim:

Fellow citizens, why do you turn and scrape every stone to gather wealth, and take so little care of your children, to whom one day you must relinquish it all?

Timeless Truth

I hated all the things I had toiled for under the sun,
because I must leave them to the one who comes after me.
And who knows whether he will be a wise man or a fool? Yet he
will have control over all the work into which I have poured my
effort and skill under the sun. This too is meaningless.

Ecclesiastes 2:18–19

A Timely Insight into . . .

Patrick Sookhdeo of Guyana, a Muslim, remembered his first contact with Christians. He felt he was intellectually superior to most, if not all, of them. He debated with them about the Trinity and blew apart their arguments. But then one day he realized, "There is more in these people than there is in me." He became a Christian.

I remember a lady from the church I pastored in Akron, Ohio, who said something like that. She was an Episcopalian, but she and her husband began attending our church because their son wanted them to visit. When I went to visit them the husband told me, "All I ever got out of church was a good nap, until I came to your church." I remember what he said, but I'll never forget what she said:

"I don't believe a thing your people believe, but I want what they've got!"

Timeless Truth

In the same way, let your light shine before men, that they may see your good deeds and praise your Father in heaven.

Matthew 5:16

A Timely Insight into . . .

Somebody remarked to the eminent philosopher Ludwig Wittgenstein how stupid medieval Europeans were. Before the birth of Copernicus, these fools looked up at the sky and thought that the sun was circling the earth, argued the critic. Just a smidgen of cosmological good sense should have convinced them that the reverse was true.

Wittgenstein is said to have replied:

"I agree. But I wonder what it would have looked like if the sun had been circling the earth."

His point was that it would look exactly the same!

Timeless Truth

So the sun stood still, and the moon stopped . . .
The sun stopped in the middle of the sky
and delayed going down about a full day.

Joshua 10:13

A Timely Insight into . . .

At times Rudyard Kipling, one of England's most distinguished writers, could be a man of few words. It was reported, once, that his publishers paid him a dollar a word for his work. Some students at Cambridge, when they heard that, sent Kipling a dollar, along with this request: "Please send us one of your very best words." Kipling replied with a one-word telegram:

"Thanks."

Years later, when Kipling was deathly sick, he stirred in his bed. The attending nurse asked, "Do you want anything?" Kipling answered,

"I want God!"

I wonder whether she was able to deliver the goods. I wonder if you would have been?

Timeless Truth

They came to Philip, who was from Bethsaida in Galilee, with a request. "Sir," they said, "we would like to see Jesus."

John 12:21

A Timely Insight into . . .

We all know only too well that little children love to ask questions. Their favorite has to be any question that starts with, "Why?" One little guy asked the ultimate "Why?" question, the one that everyone else would have, but they were afraid to ask:

"Why are all the vitamins in spinach but not in ice cream?"

Grown-ups don't ask "Why?" They ask, "Why me?" One woman who asked this grown-up version of the "Why?" question received an adult response. "In the same split second as the thought flashed through my mind, 'Why me?'," she confessed, "the question of 'Why *not* me?' reverberated in my head." Perhaps a better question than "Why should I have to suffer?" is "Why should He have had to suffer?"

Timeless Truth

Although He was a son, he learned obedience from what he suffered . . .

Hebrews 5:8

79

A Timely Insight into . . .

How would you have liked being in Ananias' shoes? Not the one that they took to the morgue after he dropped dead for telling a lie. (Although I wouldn't want to have been in his shoes, either!) I mean the one who was told by God to go see Saul of Tarsus just after his Damascus road conversion. Can you imagine being given that assignment? You might have hoped for the old Mission Impossible escape hatch, "Your mission, should you choose to accept it . . ."

But do you remember what Ananias was told concerning this Saul, who would become the great first-century missionary, Paul? God told him, "I will show him how much he must suffer for my name."

It wasn't exactly a carbon copy of the first of the *Four Spiritual Laws*, was it: "God loves you, and has a wonderful plan for your life"?

Not exactly! But Paul accepted this mission. Would you have?

Timeless Truth

*I consider that our present sufferings are not worth
comparing with the glory that will be revealed in us.*

Romans 8:18

A Timely Insight into . . .

In 1969 Neil Armstrong took his "one small step for a man, one giant leap for mankind" by stepping onto the surface of the moon. Richard Nixon was president. He was a little over-zealous in his praise of that achievement:

"The planting of human feet on the moon is the greatest moment in human history."

Billy Graham decided to set the record straight during one of his crusade meetings.

"With all due respect (to the President of the United States), the greatest moment in human history was not when man set foot on the moon, but when the infinite eternal God set foot on the earth in Jesus of Nazareth."

Timeless Truth

The Word became flesh and made his dwelling among us.

John 1:14

A Timely Insight into . . .

Arturo Toscanini had just finished conducting Beethoven's Ninth Symphony. The audience responded with a prolonged standing ovation. As the ovation began to subside, Toscanini turned toward the musicians. In a hushed voice he called, "Gentlemen, Gentlemen!" The members of the orchestra leaned forward to listen to Toscanini. He whispered audibly, "Gentlemen, I am nothing."

After a pregnant pause he added, "Gentlemen, you are nothing." Another dramatic pause. Then with great intensity, Toscanini added, "But Beethoven, he is everything, everything, everything!"

Ladies and gentlemen, I am nothing!
Ladies and gentlemen, you are nothing!
But the Lord Jesus Christ, He is everything!

Timeless Truth

So whether you eat or drink or whatever you do,
do it all for the glory of God.

1 Corinthians 10:31

A Timely Insight into . . .

Victor Hugo left a vivid account of Napoleon at the Battle of Waterloo. On the morning of the battle, the little dictator outlined his strategy for that day's campaign: "We will put the infantry here, the cavalry there, the artillery here. At the end of the day, England will be at the feet of France and Wellington will be the prisoner of Napoleon."

One of his commanders objected. "But we must not forget that man proposes but God disposes." Napoleon was furious. "I want you to understand, Sir, that Napoleon proposes and Napoleon disposes."

Victor Hugo got the last laugh:

"From that moment, Waterloo was lost, for God sent rain and hail so that the troops of Napoleon could not maneuver as he had planned, and . . .

on the night of the battle it was Napoleon who was prisoner of Wellington, and France was at the feet of England."

Timeless Truth

Pride goes before destruction, a haughty spirit before a fall.

Proverbs 16:18

A Timely Insight into . . .

During a dinner flight, a man opened his prepackaged meal and found a huge cockroach perched on his salad. When he got home, he wrote a nasty letter to the president of that airline. Days later, a special delivery letter came from the president of the company. It read:

"This was very unusual, but don't worry. I want to assure you that that particular airplane has been fumigated. In fact, all the seats and upholstery have been stripped out. We have taken disciplinary action against the stewardess who served you that meal, and she may even be fired. It is highly probable that this particular aircraft will be taken out of service. I can assure you that it will never happen again. And I trust that you will continue to fly with us."

The man was very impressed until he noticed that his own letter was stuck to the back of the president's letter. When he looked at his own letter he saw a note at the bottom that said,

"Reply with the regular roach letter."

Timeless Truth

A malicious man disguises himself with his lips,
but in his heart he harbors deceit.

Proverbs 26:24

84

A Timely Insight into . . .

George Verwer's pen dripped satire as he wrote this parody of
Onward Christian Soldiers:

Backward Christian soldiers, fleeing from the fight,
With the cross of Jesus clearly out of sight:
Christ our rightful Master stands against the foe,
But forward into battle we are chicken to go.

Like a mighty tortoise moves the church of God;
Brothers we are treading where we've often trod,
We are much divided, many bodies we,
Having different doctrines, not much charity.

Crowns and thrones may perish, kingdoms rise and wane,
But the Church of Jesus hidden does remain;
Gates of hell should never 'gainst that Church prevail,
We have Christ's own promise, but think that it will fail.

Timeless Truth

*And I tell you that you are Peter, and on this rock I will build
my church, and the gates of Hades will not overcome it.*

Matthew 16:18

A Timely Insight into . . .

It was New Year's Eve, and Tenth St. Presbyterian Church in Philadelphia was holding its annual watchnight service. Pastor Donald Grey Barnhouse was administering communion when there was a loud disturbance outside. Loud, drunken voices were heard singing:

Glorious, glorious
One keg of beer for the four of us.
Glory be to God there ain't no more of us
For heaven knows I'd drink it all alone.

Barnhouse had a mind like a steel trap. Sensing the change in mood, he seized the moment by lifting the communion cup and shouting:

Glorious, glorious
Jesus drank the dregs for all of us.
Glory be to God there is no more for us,
For on the cross He drank it all alone.

Timeless Truth

When he had received the drink, Jesus said, "It is finished."

John 19:30

A Timely Insight into . . .

Aristotle boasted about one of his works,

"This book is given for action and not for discussion."

So is the Bible!

Cho Ping was a young woman from Taiwan who visited our church in Akron one Sunday. She showed me her Chinese Bible. Her husband, Kevin, pointed out that we Americans read from left to right, shaking our heads as if to say we refuse to heed what is written. Chinese Christians, meanwhile, read up and down. It is as if they are nodding in agreement with what God's Word says.

It would appear that Chinese believers agree with Aristotle.

Timeless Truth

You have laid down precepts that are to be fully obeyed.
Oh, that my ways were steadfast in obeying your decrees!

Psalm 119:4–5

A Timely Insight into . . .

One pastor's tombstone carries the simple inscription:

"Gone to another meeting."

Apparently, this pastor had been "committee-ed" to death. (Is committee-ed a word? . . . Well, I guess it is now!) Another pastor, an old friend of mine, offered a remedy for those who are driven by their Day-Timers, like this dear brother:

On your tombstone will be the date of your birth, and the date of your death with a little dash in between. You don't have much control over either of those dates. All you can control is the little dash in between.

Timeless Truth

Who of you by worrying [or hurrying] can
add a single hour to his life?

Matthew 6:27

A Timely Insight into . . .

An old rabbi used to teach his students,

"Repent the day before you die."

"But, Rabbi," they would protest, "we don't know the day of our death."

"Then, repent today!" he would say, with a twinkle in his eye.

If that Rabbi were alive today, he would probably have to go one step further. He would have to explain what it means to repent. We moderns and post-moderns have either forgotten or never knew. I would imagine that he would have agreed with this definition:

> "Repentance is being so sorry for sin
> that you quit sinning."

Timeless Truth

"The time has come," he said. "The kingdom of God is near.
Repent and believe the good news!"

Mark 1:15

A Timely Insight into . . .

People don't die for a lie. I will never forget listening to Haddon Robinson weave this intricate argument vouching for the historicity of the resurrection of Jesus:

Men have preached a lie, knowing it's a lie if, in preaching it, they have put gold in their pockets.

Men have preached a lie, knowing it's a lie if, when preaching it, they have achieved power and authority.

But men do not preach a lie, knowing it's a lie if, every time they preach it, they are courting imprisonment, persecution, poverty, & death.

Men do not preach a lie, knowing it's a lie if, every time they preach it, they are pounding nails in their caskets.

Men do not preach a lie, knowing it's a lie, if it means that they will be crucified upside down as was Peter, or that they will be beheaded as was Paul, or that they will be stoned to death as was Stephen.

It is contrary to all human experience for men to go out and spend their lives preaching a lie, knowing it's a lie, if every time they preach it, they are ostracized from the community, hounded by the authorities, and turned into the laughing-stock of society.

And yet that is precisely the penalty the early Christians paid for preaching the resurrection.

Timeless Truth

For what I received I passed on to you as of first importance: that Christ died for our sins according to the Scriptures, that he was buried, that he was raised on the third day according to the Scriptures, and that he appeared to Peter, and then to the Twelve.

1 Corinthians 15:3–5

A Timely Insight into . . .

A young guy bought his girlfriend an orchid. It was the first orchid he had ever purchased and the first one she had ever received. There was a card with the orchid which read,

"With all my love, and most of my allowance."

A father complained all the way home about the church service. "The sermon was too long, the music was too loud, and the lights were too dim." His eight-year old boy said,

"Dad, it didn't seem like a bad show for a dollar."

Perhaps that father should send God an orchid with a card that reads,

"With little of my love, and even less of my allowance."

Timeless Truth

Do everything without complaining or arguing, so that you may become blameless and pure, children of God without fault in a crooked and depraved generation . . .

Philippians 2:14–15

A Timely Insight into . . .

Howard Hendricks, Dallas Seminary's favorite "prof," recalls:

My family and I were awakened some time ago in the middle of the night with the crash of glass and with the most unearthly screams I've ever heard. We rushed to the front of our home to see our neighbor's house going up in fire. My two sons and I rushed across the street and arrived just in time to see the last member of the family coming through the window. We melted back into the crowd that was gathering. I saw a pitiful sight. I saw a very, very educated and sophisticated man take his fists and clench them and beat that sod with all of his might, cursing the fire department, cursing God, cursing everybody, because his home had gone up in smoke. And as my two sons and I melted into that crowd, I said to them,

"Men, what would we have lost, had that been our home?"

Timeless Truth

Then he said to them, "Watch out! Be on your guard against all kinds of greed; a man's life does not consist in the abundance of his possessions."

Luke 12:15

A Timely Insight into . . .

For several years, we had father-and-son breakfasts at our church. The sons were asked to write down the one question they would most like to ask their dads. Here are some of the responses. Are you sitting down?

Why are you never home?

How can I become a Christian?

I would ask him why he became a Christian.

Will you still love me if I make a mistake in life?

Do I show enough love? or Do I show love to you?

Dad, what is my purpose on earth and why did you want me —or did you?

Timeless Truth

The father of a righteous man has great joy;
he who has a wise son delights in him.

Proverbs 23:24

A Timely Insight into . . .

Some people think that the "Golden Rule" is too tough. Like the dollar, they would prefer to be set loose from the gold standard. One pastor offered these substitutes, with tongue-in-cheek:

Silver **Rule — "Do unto others as they have already done unto you."**

Iron **Rule — "Do unto others as you fully expect them to do unto you."**

Bronze **Rule — "Do unto others before they do unto you."**

Copper **Rule — Do unto others—and cut out."**

Timeless Truth

Do to others as you would have them do to you.

Luke 6:31

A Timely Insight into . . .

Samuel Morse invented the telegraph, which is why the Morse Code was named for him. A reporter once asked Morse, "Did you come to a place in trying to invent the telegraph where you didn't know what to do? If so, what did you do to achieve a break-through?" Morse replied,

"I asked God."

"Did God give you the knowledge you needed?" the reporter asked. "Yes," Morse responded. "That's why I felt I never deserved the honors that have come to me from Europe and America because of the invention associated with my name. I have made a valuable application of the use of electrical power, but it was all through God's help. It wasn't because I was superior to other scientists. When the Lord wanted to bestow this gift on mankind, He had to use someone. I'm just grateful He chose to reveal it through me."

No wonder the first message to cross the wire was,

"What hath God wrought?"

Timeless Truth

Who is wise and understanding among you?
Let him show it by his good life, by deeds done in the
humility that comes from wisdom.

James 3:13

A Timely Insight into . . .

The Lone Ranger and Tonto were riding across the plains when off to the west they noticed a cloud of dust. It turned out to be a band of Indians galloping directly at them. They turned their horses around and headed east. Pretty soon they saw another thick cloud of dust in front of them. More Indians. They turned their horses north. But another cloud of dust revealed more Indians. In desperation they turned their horses south and galloped off in that direction. Once again, a choking cloud of dust revealed more Indians attacking from that direction.

Realizing they were surrounded, the Lone Ranger looked at Tonto and asked, "What do we do now, Tonto?" Tonto glared back at him.

"What do you mean 'we,' Paleface?"

Talk about being an Indian giver, eh?

Timeless Truth

A friend loves at all times,
and a brother is born for adversity.

Proverbs 17:17

A Timely Insight into . . .

Are you familiar with the Continental Divide? It is a ridge that runs the length of North America (north and south). If a raindrop falls a centimeter west of that Divide, it will flow toward the Pacific. If it falls a centimeter to the east of that Divide, it will flow until it reaches the Mississippi River Valley and out into the Gulf of Mexico, eventually reaching the Atlantic Ocean.

Both drops start to flow from almost the same spot on the same peak—only a couple centimeters apart. But they end up oceans apart!

The same thing happens within families. Two children start with the same background, the same opportunity, very similar genes and chromosomes, the same tendencies and abilities, yet they end up miles apart.

Timeless Truth

*The father of a righteous man has great joy; he who has
a wise son delights in him. May your father and
mother be glad; may she who gave you birth rejoice!*

Proverbs 23:24–25

A Timely Insight into . . .

An old missionary, who was battling cancer, had this tacked up on the bulletin board by his bed in his hospital room:

What cancer cannot do:
> **It cannot cripple love**
> **It cannot shatter hope**
> **It cannot corrode faith**
> **It cannot eat away peace**
> **It cannot destroy confidence**
> **It cannot kill friendship**
> **It cannot shut out memories**
> **It cannot silence courage**
> **It cannot invade the soul**
> **It cannot quench the Spirit**
> **It cannot lessen the power of the resurrection!**

Timeless Truth

But we have this treasure in jars of clay to show that this all-surpassing power is from God and not from us.

2 Corinthians 4:7

A Timely Insight into . . .

For a Father's Day message several years ago I generated this list of lessons, which I titled,

What I've learned in 12 years as a dad

I'm not as good a father as I once thought I would be.

You can never afford to have children, so you should go ahead and have them.

Parenting = discipleship. (My home is a training camp for my daughters' lives and minds.)

It is important for me to say "I'm sorry!" to my girls when I've been out of line.

Spending "quality time" with my kids is easier said than done.

My biggest surprise: The feeling I have for my own children is unlike the feeling I have for any other person. It is a unique love.

The capacity for my children to hurt me deeply is very great.

Hugging my girls and telling them "I love you" is critical.

It is imperative for me to tell my children what I appreciate about them, with as many specifics as possible.

Negative jabs like "You're no good!" or "You'll never amount to anything!" are destructive.

When I have spanked Rachel and Julie, I have found that it really does hurt me more than it hurts them.

The only goal I have for my girls is that they walk with God all the days of their lives.

You never retire from being a parent.

Timeless Truth

Unless the LORD builds the house, its builders labor in vain. Unless the LORD watches over the city, the watchmen stand guard in vain.

Psalm 127:1

A Timely Insight into . . .

I was running on the beach in South Carolina with my brother-in-law, Duane. As we jogged he started telling me about people he was trying to help, people he genuinely cared about. Then he said to me,

"I believe the most important thing in life is to love your neighbor as yourself."

I interrupted,

"You know, Duane, that certainly is important. But Jesus said there was one thing even more important than that."

Naturally, he asked, "What's that?"

"Well, Jesus said you must love God with all your heart, soul, mind, and strength."

"That's the part I don't do so good at," he admitted. Duane was not a Christian at the time. But . . .

Timeless Truth

Jesus replied: "'Love the Lord your God with all your heart and with all your soul and with all your mind.' This is the first and greatest commandment."

Matthew 22:37

A Timely Insight into . . .

This great verse was originally addressed to Israel. Its immediate application was to the nation of Israel in Jeremiah's day. However, it has been borrowed by many believers today during troubling times, and applied to their pressing circumstances. I know, because recently I have been signing my letters,

"Living by Jeremiah 29:11"

I believe this promise can be applied to believers today without violating the truth of the text. After all, God who spoke that promise to the nation of Israel has not changed. He is the same yesterday, today, and forever (just like His Son!). Jeremiah 29:11 represents the tender loving care of God. It can apply to a Christian today because God loves believers today at least as much as He loved the nation of Israel in Jeremiah's day.

Timeless Truth

"For I know the plans I have for you," declares the LORD,
"plans to prosper you and not to harm you,
plans to give you hope and a future."

Jeremiah 29:11

A Timely Insight into . . .

Jesus is the patron saint of nobodies: the billions of nameless and faceless people of this world.

The scarlet woman in John 4 is nameless and faceless. The cripple who had suffered for 38 years with a disease and was healed by Jesus in John 5 was not identified by name. The blind man in John 9, likewise, is an anonymous face in a crowd of people healed in the Gospels. The thief on the cross has no name.

There is no need for us to have a tomb for the "Unknown Christian."

The number of nameless and faceless people in the Gospels is the trademark of our Savior's impressive love for ordinary people.

Timeless Truth

The blind receive sight, the lame walk, those who have leprosy are cured, the deaf hear, the dead are raised, and the good news is preached to the poor.

Luke 7:22

A Timely Insight into . . .

In Revelation 21:6 God says the water of life comes "without cost." So does everything else in heaven, including your condo. (The old King James word, "mansion," would be the equivalent of a condominium today, not an English Tudor mansion.) That means there will be:

no down payment,
no realtor fees,
no closing costs,
no mortgage payments,
no property tax,
no utility bills, and
no fear of foreclosure.

Since there is no sickness, there will be no hospitals. Since there is no death, there will be no cemeteries. And since there is no sin, there will be no regret!

Timeless Truth

To him who is thirsty I will give to drink without cost
from the spring of the water of life.

Revelation 21:6

A Timely Insight into . . .

In the Sunday paper several years ago, there was an intriguing item that caught my attention. The headline for the piece reads,

"Dino dung sells for $4,500 in London."

In light of the recent success of Jurassic Park and Barney, the dinosaur, "dinosaur pies" are apparently hot stuff. The article includes these two paragraphs that give the details of the purchase:

Twenty-three pieces of fossilized dinosaur dung, scooped from around Hanksville, Utah, recently sold for $4,500 at a London auction house.

Owner Jan Stobbe, a Dutch geologist, said the dung sold to an unidentified British buyer for 10 times as much as he thought it was worth.

Timeless Truth

What is more, I consider everything a loss compared
to the surpassing greatness of knowing Christ Jesus
my Lord, for whose sake I have lost all things.
I consider them rubbish, that I may gain Christ.

Philippians 3:8

A Timely Insight into . . .

There are two critical ingredients in the recipe of life:

"the game of life" and "the Lord of life."

The question is, are we willing to play the game according to His rules?

An equally valid question for perfectly modern millennialists is this:

"How have we crowded God out of the center of our lives?"

Floyd McClung offered this vicious reply:

"By replacing Him with ourselves."

Ah, yes. The 21st Century Trinity: "Me, Myself, and I!"

Timeless Truth

You shall have no other gods before me.

Exodus 20:3

A Timely Insight into . . .

Alexander Maclaren, a Scot, described grace as "a kind of shorthand for the whole sum of unmerited blessings which come to men through Jesus Christ. GRACE means the unconditioned, undeserved, spontaneous, eternal, stooping, pardoning love of God."

A popular acronym spells out G–R–A–C–E as "God's Riches at Christ's Expense." That is quite true and quite clever. But consider this. It is quite true and quite convicting.

Grace means that we get just the opposite of what we deserve.

Robert Louis Stevenson was right. We breathe by grace! "Everything's grace. We walk upon it, we breathe it, we live and die by it, it makes the nails and axles of the universe!"

Timeless Truth

And God is able to make all grace abound to you, so that in all things at all times, having all that you need, you will abound in every good work.

2 Corinthians 9:8

A Timely Insight into . . .

A poor man stopped by our church in Akron in the middle of the week to get help. He had been divorced twice, he was out of work, and he needed financial assistance. As we talked, I was fascinated by his life story. You might find it interesting, too.

He was not a Christian. He had a horrible case of "religious schizophrenia." His mother had tried to gas him to death to keep him from the sinful world. For a brief time he had attended the Chapel in Akron when Carl Burnham, the founding pastor, was still alive.

In 1961 Carl Burnham died. But just two or three days before he died, he had given this young man a Bible. In the flyleaf of that Bible, Burnham wrote:

"READ IT, BELIEVE IT, AND DIE BY IT."

If only this dear man had taken that great advice!

Timeless Truth

How can a young man keep his way pure?
By living according to your word.

Psalm 119:9

109

A Timely Insight into . . .

William J. O'Malley's words cut to the chase:

> "Quite unlike Hitler, or the Stones, or Hefner—who also changed the world simply by discerning which way the parade was heading and getting in front of it—Jesus did not give us a message we wanted to hear. He came to turn the parade in precisely the opposite direction; he spoke words hard for our canny hearts even to give credence to, much less heed: take the last place (the real parade is heading the other way), forget yourself (even your shortcomings), take up your cross, heal the hateful."

Isn't it sad that Thomas à Kempis' words have never been more true?

Jesus now has many lovers of His heavenly kingdom, but few bearers of His cross.

Timeless Truth

Then Jesus said to his disciples,
"If anyone would come after me, he must
deny himself and take up his cross and follow me."

Matthew 16:24

A Timely Insight into . . .

At a gathering of the National Association of Evangelicals in Columbus, Ohio, I heard a spokesman for Love-in-Action talk about his ministry to people who were dying of AIDS. His testimony concerning some of those patients who had become Christians sparkled:

"I can say without a doubt that some of the greatest Christians I have ever met are dying of AIDS."

He clarified his dazzling comment when he added:

"These are people who have no materialistic ambitions in life. Their only desire is to know Jesus, and through the remainder of their days, to make Him known. It's people like that who inspire us and keep us going."

Timeless Truth

I eagerly expect and hope that I will in no way be ashamed, but will have sufficient courage so that now as always Christ will be exalted in my body, whether by life or by death.

Philippians 1:20

A Timely Insight into . . .

Reflecting on the staggering comment in 1 Corinthians 6:19–20, I jotted down these three thoughts to amplify a sound point:

1. **Your time is not your own.** You have been bought with a price; therefore, glorify God in your body by the use of your time.

2. **Your talent is not your own.** You have been bought with a price; therefore, glorify God in your body by the use of your talents.

3. **Your treasury is not your own.** You have been bought with a price; therefore, glorify God in your body by the use of your treasury.

Timeless Truth

You are not your own; you were bought at a price.
Therefore honor God with your body.

1 Corinthians 6:19–20

A Timely Insight into . . .

I can't remember who said it, but I can remember what he said:

> "I know Jesus tells us in the Bible to feed His sheep. He even tells us to feed His lambs. But nowhere can I recall that He tells us to feed His giraffes."

That reminds me of a comment a friend made to me about one of my seminary professors. After hearing my professor preach, he gave me his impression of what he had heard. My friend was not an oxymoron, but what he said probably is:

"He was an excellent speaker. I hardly understood what He was saying."

Timeless Truth

For Christ did not send me to baptize, but to preach the gospel—not with words of human wisdom, lest the cross of Christ be emptied of its power.

1 Corinthians 1:17

A Timely Insight into . . .

Thornton Wilder probably gave expression to his own belief when he put these words into the mouth of one of his characters:

> "I don't care what they say with their mouths—everybody knows that something is eternal. And it ain't houses and it ain't names, and it ain't earth, and it ain't even stars—everybody knows in their bones that something is eternal, and that something has to do with human beings. All the greatest people ever lived have been telling us that for five thousand years and yet you'd be surprised how people are always losing hold of it. There's something way down deep that's eternal about every human being."

Thornton Wilder was right!

**Everybody lives forever
. . . one place or another!**

Timeless Truth

Enter through the narrow gate. For wide is the gate and broad is the road that leads to destruction, and many enter through it. But small is the gate and narrow the road that leads to life, and only a few find it.

Matthew 7:13–14

A Timely Insight into . . .

Somebody in Chicago told evangelist Billy Sunday:

> "If I could have all I wanted of any one thing,
> I would take money."

Doesn't leave much room for God, does it? Nor does this:

> "Money isn't everything . . .
> but it sure beats whatever is in second place."

Back in 1981 or 1982, when gold was still a high-priced commodity, Geraldo Rivera introduced a 20/20 segment with this shocking claim:

"There aren't many absolutes in this world anymore, but tonight's feature is all about one of them . . . GOLD."

So there is still at least one absolute, eh, Geraldo?

Timeless Truth

For where your treasure is, there your heart will be also.

Matthew 6:21

A Timely Insight into . . .

During a conference attended by many leading churchmen and scientists, Albert Einstein read a paper in which he suggested:

> "In their struggle for the ethical good, teachers of religion must have the stature to give up the doctrine of a personal god."

But, what do "teachers of religion" have to offer to ethics without the notion of a Personal God? Didn't Einstein ever read what Dostoyevsky wrote? "If God didn't exist, everything would be permissible." There is no right and wrong if there is no God. Dostoyevsky was right, which means that Einstein was wrong.

In his autobiography, *Out of My Later Years*, Einstein wrote:

"Science without religion is lame, religion without science is blind."

Obviously, Einstein was no friend of God or of people who believe in God. But as a German Jew who barely escaped the Nazi holocaust, he found it necessary to make this surprising confession:

"Only the Church stood squarely across the path of Hitler's campaign for suppressing truth. I never had any special interest in the Church before, but now I feel a great affection and admiration, because the Church alone has had the courage and persistence to stand for intellectual truth and moral freedom. I am forced thus to confess that what I once despised I now praise unreservedly."

Wasn't Germany a leader in scientific technology in the 1930s and 40s? Nazi Germany demonstrates that science without religion is lame! To paraphrase H.G. Wells, it is like a boot, goose-stepping on a human face forever. And religion without science isn't blind. It just needs to wear faith like some people need to wear eye-glasses.

Timeless Truth

Yet he did not waver through unbelief regarding the promise of God, but was strengthened in his faith and gave glory to God . . .

Romans 4:20

A Timely Insight into . . .

He loved to watch his two Irish setters romp in his backyard. Then, one day a little bulldog broke through the fence. With pride, the man looked on as his two dogs defended their turf. At the end of the skirmish, the little bulldog slipped outside the fence, licking its wounds.

But the very next day, the bulldog returned. A fierce dogfight resumed, a jumble of teeth, hair, and eyes. Once again the setters proved to be the masters of their own turf.

Day after day, the bulldog came back, eager to battle. To the dismay of their owner, the day came when the setters saw the bulldog coming, and dashed to the house. While they whined to be let inside, the bulldog strutted around the yard like King Tut.

Talk about bulldog tenacity!

Timeless Truth

*Therefore, since we are surrounded by such
a great cloud of witnesses, . . . let us run with
perseverance the race marked out for us.*

Hebrews 12:1

A Timely Insight into . . .

A friend once reminded President Ulysses S. Grant that Senator Charles Sumner of Massachusetts did not believe in the Bible.

"Of course Sumner doesn't believe in the Bible," answered Grant. "He didn't write it."

Thomas Paine didn't just refuse to believe the Bible. He attacked it with glee in The Age of Reason. But when Paine showed his manuscript to Ben Franklin, Mr. Franklin advised him not to publish it, saying,

"The world is bad enough with the Bible; what would it be without it?"

Timeless Truth

Heaven and earth will pass away, but my words will never pass away.

Mark 13:31

A Timely Insight into . . .

Rome was center stage in the first century. Jesus was just an extra in the crowd, hidden from the view of the audience. But, oh, how time has rearranged the players! As someone has said, most people would never have heard of Pontius Pilate, a symbol of the might of Rome, if it were not for his celebrated prisoner, Jesus Christ.

George Bernard Shaw captured some of that irony in his play, On the Rocks. He added some imaginary dialogue to the noteworthy conversation between Pilate and his prisoner. In Shaw's re-creation, Jesus gets the famous last word:

"The kingdom of God is striving to come. The empire that looks backward in terror shall give way to the kingdom that looks forward with hope."

Timeless Truth

"Do you refuse to speak to me?" Pilate said.
"Don't you realize I have power either to free you or to crucify you?" Jesus answered, "You would have no power over me if it were not given to you from above."

John 19:10–11

A Timely Insight into . . .

In the third century, a man named Cyprian wrote to a friend some words that still strike terror into the pit of hell:

This seems a cheerful world, Donatus, when I view it from this fair garden, under the shadow of these vines. But if I climbed some great mountain and looked out over the wide lands, you know very well what I would see. Brigands on the high roads, pirates of the seas, in the amphitheaters men murdered to please the applauding crowds, under all roofs misery and selfishness.

It is really a bad world, Donatus, an incredibly bad world. Yet in the midst of it I have found a quiet and holy people. They have discovered a joy which is a thousand times better than any pleasure of this sinful life. They are despised and persecuted, but they care not. They have overcome the world. These people, Donatus, are the Christians—and I am one of them.

Timeless Truth

Who is it that overcomes the world?
Only he who believes that Jesus is the Son of God.

1 John 5:5

A Timely Insight into . . .

Don't you just love BC, the comic strip with the ever-present boulders? In one, the rock is inscribed "Trivia Test," and BC is tossing out questions to one of his prehistoric pals. "Here's one from the Bible," he mutters.

"What were the last words uttered by Lot's wife?"

Without giving it much thought, the other caveman answered,

"The heck with your fanatical beliefs, I'm going to take one last look!"

And we all know what happened to Mrs. Lot. She could be one of the pillars of the Morton Salt Company.

Timeless Truth

Jesus replied, "No one who puts his hand to the plow and looks back is fit for service in the kingdom of God."

Luke 9:62

A Timely Insight into . . .

Art Linkletter will always be remembered for his features with children. "Kids Say the Darndest Things!" Linkletter would say. Here are a couple of the many funny things kids said about popular Bible stories.

One little boy was asked, "What is your favorite Bible Story?" He replied, Adam and Eve." Linkletter then asked, "What lesson do we learn from that story?" Quick as a flash the boy warned,

"Never trust a woman. If you listen to a woman you'll end up going to hell."

Another child, when asked the same question, responded, "Jesus turning water into wine." When asked, "What lesson do we learn from that story?" the little guy said,

"When you run out of wine, get on your knees and pray."

Timeless Truth

. . . and the master of the banquet tasted the water that had been turned into wine. . . . Then he called the bridegroom aside and said, "Everyone brings out the choice wine first and then the cheaper wine after the guests have had too much to drink; but you have saved the best till now."

John 2:9–10

A Timely Insight into . . .

A Texan went to Alaska and was impressed by the size of the state. He walked into a barbershop and asked, "What do I do to become a citizen of this here state?

The barber told him that he would need to shave his head, kill a grizzly bear, and kiss an Eskimo. The Texan thought that sounded pretty reasonable, so he dropped down into the barber's chair to get his head shaved. Then he left to carry out the other two requirements. When he finally returned to the barbershop, splattered with blood from head to toe, he asked,

"O.K., now where is that Eskimo I'm supposed to shoot?"

Aren't we all a little like that? We keep getting the instructions wrong.

Timeless Truth

He who scorns instruction will pay for it,
but he who respects a command is rewarded.

Proverbs 13:13

A Timely Insight into . . .

Oscar Wilde used to love to tell a miserable parable. It went something like this: Jesus was walking through the streets of the city. In an open courtyard, he saw a man he had healed partying with his friends. "Sir," said Jesus, "Why do you live like that?"

"I was a leper," said the young man, "and you healed me. You live only once, so you've got to grab for all the gusto you can. What's wrong with that?"

Then he saw a young hooker dressed quite provocatively. "Young lady," Jesus said to the girl, "Why do you dress that way?"

"I'm a sinner, and you forgave me. So why not sin more, so grace can abound more?"

Timeless Truth

What shall we say, then? Shall we go on sinning so that grace may increase? By no means! We died to sin; how can we live in it any longer?

Romans 6:1–2

A Timely Insight into . . .

Expert opinions are sometimes news. This one is not news, but it is noteworthy because of who said it:

Children now live in luxury, they have bad manners, contempt for authority; they show disrespect for elders and love to chatter in place of exercise. Children are now tyrants of the household. They no longer rise when an elder enters the room and they contradict their parents. They chatter before company, gobble up the food at the table, they cross their legs and tyrannize their teachers.

Believe it or not, those were the words of Socrates, the ancient Greek philosopher.

Timeless Truth

But mark this: There will be terrible times in the last days. People will be lovers of themselves, lovers of money, boastful, proud, abusive, disobedient to their parents . . .

2 Timothy 3:1–2

A Timely Insight into . . .

One pastor complained that his men were backing out of their commitments to the church. It was as if they were changing the words of the hymn from "Take my life and let it be" to

Take my wife and let me be!

Edgar A. Guest noticed the same problem in his day and captured it in this bit of verse:

> Leave it to the ministers,
>   And soon the church will die;
>
> Leave it to the women folk,
>   And some will pass it by.

Timeless Truth

I looked for a man among them who would build up the wall and stand before me in the gap on behalf of the land so I would not have to destroy it, but I found none.

Ezekiel 22:30

A Timely Insight into . . .

What do most people associate with "meekness"? How about words like "doormat," or "wimp," or "wallflower." In the minds of most Americans it is a simple grammatical equation. Meekness = Weakness.

Some people think that meekness is a joke. Like the guy who said,

> "Yesterday I told one of the meekest people I know that he would inherit the earth. . . . He asked me for a second choice."

Or the domineering wife in the cartoon who snapped at her mousy husband,

> "If the meek inherit the Earth, you ought to be in line for a couple thousand acres."

But one young coed wasn't joking when she snapped,

> "You and I both know that the meek get ground into the earth."

If that's what you think, then I dare you to take the "meekness challenge":

"If you think meekness is weakness, then try being meek for a week."

Timeless Truth

Blessed are the meek, for they will inherit the earth.

Matthew 5:5

A Timely Insight into . . .

Under the skin, hypocrisy and flattery are twins. The only difference is:

> . . . a hypocrite will say behind your back what he will not say to your face, while a flatterer will say to your face what he will not say behind your back.

Flattery, like hypocrisy, can be a deadly trap. As Howard Hendricks loved to remind us:

"Man is the only creature that you can pat on the back and his head swells up. Praise is like perfume; it's good to smell, but I wouldn't recommend swallowing it."

Timeless Truth

Whoever flatters his neighbor is spreading a net for his feet.

Proverbs 29:5

A Timely Insight into . . .

Tim Hansel discovered what he describes as a "tremendous formula for success." It consists of only ten points, which are easy to remember (as you can easily see):

1. Pray

2. Work

3. Pray

4. Work

5. Pray

6. Work

7. Pray

8. Work

9. Pray

10. Work

To summarize: Success is part our part, and part God's part.

Timeless Truth

. . . continue to work out your salvation with fear and trembling, for it is God who works in you to will and to act according to his good purpose.

Philippians 2:12–13

A Timely Insight into . . .

During a series of revival meetings conducted by the evangelist R.A. Torrey many years ago, there was no response to the invitation the first several nights. Homer Hammontree, Torrey's songleader, was frustrated by the lukewarm crowds.

"Ham," the evangelist replied, "It is required in stewards that a man be found faithful. Good night; I am going to bed."

Then one night during the service, there was a tremendous outpouring of God's Spirit and a great response to the invitation. Hammontree was exuberant. Torrey said quietly,

"Ham, it is required in stewards that a man be found faithful. Good night; I am going to bed."

Timeless Truth

Now it is required that those who have been given a trust must prove faithful.

1 Corinthians 4:2

A Timely Insight into . . .

Leave it to Ralph Waldo Emerson to say something with a few short, meaningful words that will have a long shelf life. In his essay "Prudence," written around 1841, he wrote:

> "Do what we can, summer will have its flies.
> If we walk in the woods, we must feed mosquitoes."

William Bradford, the governor of the Plymouth Colony, might not have been happy with Emerson's pasteurized expression. But he, too, believed, like Robert Louis Stevenson, that "Everybody sooner or later sits down to a banquet of consequences." Bradford wrote:

"Those who believe in the Holy Scriptures are bound to observe its teachings. Those who do not are to be bound by its consequences."

Timeless Truth

This is love for God: to obey his commands.
And his commands are not burdensome . . .

1 John 5:3

A Timely Insight into . . .

W.P. Nicholson, an old Irish evangelist, preached in Belfast, Ireland, when that city was the major shipbuilding capital of the world. The men from the shipyards would lay down their tools as soon as the horn sounded at the end of the day. They would form lines and march out of the shipyards, parading through the streets straight to the church where the evangelist was preaching. They filled the church, still dressed in their work clothes. Then Nicholson would preach to them another convicting sermon, calling for repentance. Many men accepted Christ and started to bring back everything they had stolen from the shipyards. They were "Exhibit A" of fruit worthy to repentance! Finally, the bosses of the shipyards had to make a public request,

"Will those men attending the meetings of Mr. W.P. Nicholson please stop returning stolen goods. We have nowhere to store them."

Timeless Truth

Godly sorrow brings repentance that leads to salvation and leaves no regret, but worldly sorrow brings death.

2 Corinthians 7:10

A Timely Insight into . . .

Spiritual laws are as fixed as natural laws. The law of gravity is no more real than the law of sowing and reaping. When Jesus told a woman of ill-repute that "Everyone who drinks of this water shall thirst again," He was enacting a new spiritual law. It is a law that covers almost every sphere of life today. In effect, Jesus was saying . .

Everyone who swallows dollar bills will thirst for more.

Everyone who gulps sexual pleasure will thirst for more.

Everyone who sips political power will thirst for more.

Everyone who slurps at fame will thirst for more.

Timeless Truth

Jesus answered, "Everyone who drinks this water will be thirsty again, but whoever drinks the water I give him will never thirst. Indeed, the water I give him will become in him a spring of water welling up to eternal life."

John 4:13–14

A Timely Insight into . . .

One Sunday night I heard a radio broadcast of a church service in the Detroit area. I don't remember much about the preacher, but I do remember what he preached about. During his sermon he invited people to receive a "blessing." He assured his audience,

"You'll get it right away!"

I don't doubt that someone got a "blessing" right away. But not the members of his audience. This modern-day Elmer Gantry hawked these "blessings" shamelessly.

Bring $10 and get two kinds of oil: "Lightning oil" and "Get-it-now oil."

Listeners were guaranteed that everything they wanted would flow their way. I don't doubt that everything flowed directly to his bank account.

Timeless Truth

"Watch out for false prophets. They come to you in sheep's clothing, but inwardly they are ferocious wolves."

Matthew 7:15

A Timely Insight into . . .

Crosses are popular. People wear them on necklaces, as earrings, and even as tattoos. But crosses were not status symbols in the first century. They were instruments of exquisite torture for rebels, criminals, slaves, and other lowlifes. John Stott reminds us:

"Roman citizens were exempt from crucifixion, except in extreme cases of treason."

Cicero, the famous Roman statesman and orator of the first century, in one of his speeches, described crucifixion in no uncertain terms as

> "a most cruel and disgusting punishment."

To be perfectly clear, he spelled out his strong feelings about the exemption that belonged to the citizens of Rome:

> "To bind a Roman citizen is a crime, to flog him is an abomination, to kill him is almost an act of murder: to crucify him is—What? There is no fitting word that can possibly describe so horrible a deed."

Again, Cicero, in defending one of Rome's senators who had been charged with murder, did not mince words:

"Let the very name of the cross be far, not only from the body of a Roman citizen, but even from his thoughts, his eyes, his ears. . . . indeed the mere mention of [crucifixion] is unworthy of a Roman citizen and a free man.

For Jews there was an extra dose of shame that came packaged with crucifixion. The Law spelled out that anyone hanged on a tree was cursed. No wonder Jesus despised being nailed on a Roman cross.

Timeless Truth

Let us fix our eyes on Jesus, the author and perfecter of our faith, who for the joy set before him endured the cross, scorning its shame, and sat down at the right hand of the throne of God.

Hebrews 12:2

A Timely Insight into . . .

Did you ever notice how Jesus treated His friends (He had called them "friends" that very night) who failed Him so miserably in the Garden of Gethsemane? Do you remember what He was expecting from them? All He asked them to do was stay alert while He slipped away to wrestle with God in prayer. But what did they do? Probably the same thing you and I would have done, if we had been in their sandals. They fell asleep. More than once! He woke them after one hour in prayer and asked them to stay awake this time. But, true to form, they snoozed. Yet His next words to them were, "Rise, let us go!" They abandoned Him, but He would never abandon them. As someone has said,

"He walked with failures as if they had never failed."

If you choose to walk with Jesus down the road of life, you will discover the same thing. He walks with failures as if they had never failed.

Timeless Truth

Jesus Christ is the same yesterday and today and forever.

Hebrews 13:8

A Timely Insight into . . .

Monday Night Football was on, so all the rest of the world was on hold. Howard Cosell was still doing some of the play-by-play (which gives you some idea of how long ago this was). Cosell was forging through the crowd in the stadium and stumbled across George Foreman, the former heavy-weight champion. At half-time, Cosell was featured on camera for an impromptu interview with Foreman. He asked George if he planned to get back in the ring. (This was light-years before Foreman staged his recent comeback in the ring.)

Foreman explained that he was now preaching in a church, and that he no longer had an interest in boxing. Then he added this punch line, which nearly decked Cosell,

"No, Howard, Jesus is my boss!"

Timeless Truth

For we do not preach ourselves, but Jesus Christ as Lord,
and ourselves as your servants for Jesus' sake.

2 Corinthians 4:5

A Timely Insight into . . .

A little boy had been very naughty and his mother had given him a spanking. For the rest of the evening the desire for revenge rankled in his little head. At bedtime he knelt by his bed and said his prayers. He prayed for every member of the family by name, except one. When he got up from his knees, he looked at his mother with a devious eye and as he crawled into bed he said,

"I suppose that you noticed you were not in it."

Jesus did not pray like that, He included everyone in the Family of God in His prayer.

Timeless Truth

"My prayer is not for them alone. I pray also for those who will believe in me through their message, that all of them may be one, Father, just as you are in me and I am in you. May they also be in us so that the world may believe that you have sent me."

John 17:20–21

A Timely Insight into . . .

Charles Spurgeon, the great British preacher of the 19th century, carried a letter in his pocket to the pulpit. It was written by a man who was well-educated and successful. But he was an agnostic in his BC (before Christ) days. In fact, Spurgeon said, he was "a sarcastic agnostic," a man who took pleasure in grinding the things of God into the dust. But, that was in the past. In his letter he told how Spurgeon's ministry had changed his life. Here was his analysis of what he was BC:

**"I was without happiness for this life,
and without hope for the next."**

Please notice: the key word in any testimony is "was." What we were, we are not now.

Timeless Truth

*Remember that at that time you were separate
from Christ, excluded from citizenship in Israel and
foreigners to the covenants of the promise,
without hope and without God in the world.*
Ephesians 2:12

A Timely Insight into . . .

W.A. Criswell served as pastor of First Baptist Church of Dallas, Texas for more than 50 years. How did he stay there so long? Could this be his secret?

I preach that Jesus is

>> **personally,**

>>> **visibly,**

>>>> **actually,**

>>>>> **truly,**

>>>>>> **really**

>>>>>>> **coming again.**

I believe the promise of the angels in Acts 1

>>>> **word for word,**

>>>>> **syllable for syllable,**

>>>>>> **letter by letter.**

Timeless Truth

"Men of Galilee," they said, "why do you stand here looking into the sky? This same Jesus, who has been taken from you into heaven, will come back in the same way you have seen him go into heaven."

Acts 1:11

A Timely Insight into . . .

A friend of mine called me one day while we were being buried by a blizzard in Akron, Ohio. He was taking advantage of the time off to further his goal to read through the New Testament. As he read, he stumbled across a statement in Colossians 1:15 that jumped off the page and into his imagination. My friend was eager to tell me what he had discovered. He asked me, "Do you understand what this means?" Then he proceeded to tell me, in words that I will never forget:

"When God looks in the mirror He sees Jesus Christ."

Timeless Truth

He is the image of the invisible God,
the firstborn over all creation.

Colossians 1:15

A Timely Insight into . . .

In one of his stories, William Thackeray, the English writer, told about the death of one of his characters, old Colonel Newcome.

Just before his passing, at the usual evening hour, the chapel bell of the school nearby began to toll. The old colonel's hands, outside the bed covers, feebly beat time. Just as the last bell struck, a sweet smile lighted up his face; and, lifting his head a little, he said, "Adsum" and fell back.

***Adsum* is a Latin word. It means "present."**

It was the word that boys in the school used when they answered the daily roll call in class. Colonel Newcome, though a frail old man, still had the heart of a child. When the roll is called up yonder, he knew he would be there.

Timeless Truth

Surely goodness and love will follow me all the days of my life,
and I will dwell in the house of the LORD forever.

Psalm 23:6

A Timely Insight into . . .

A World War II fighter pilot left behind these courageous words:

> **Almighty and all present Power,**
> **Short is the prayer I make to Thee,**
> **I do not ask in battle hour**
> **For any shield to cover me.**
> **The vast unalterable way,**
> **From which the stars do not depart**
> **May not be turned aside to stay**
> **The bullet flying to my heart.**
> **But this I pray, be at my side**
> **When death is drawing through the sky.**
> **Almighty God who also died,**
> **Teach me the way that I should die.**

Timeless Truth

"I eagerly expect and hope that I will in no way be ashamed,
but will have sufficient courage so that now as always Christ
will be exalted in my body, whether by life or by death."

Philippians 1:20

A Timely Insight into . . .

Michael Denton, a molecular biologist and an atheist (with no theological axe to grind), has dared to question science's sacred cow, evolution:

> The human brain consists of about ten thousand million nerve cells. Each nerve cell puts out somewhere in the region of between ten thousand and one hundred thousand connecting fibres by which it makes contact with other nerve cells in the brain. Altogether the total number of connections in the human brain approaches 10 [to the 15th power] or a thousand million million. Numbers in the order of 10 [to the 15th power] are of course completely beyond comprehension. Imagine an area about half the size of the USA (one million square miles) covered in a forest of trees containing ten thousand trees per square mile. If each tree contained one hundred thousand leaves, the total number of leaves in the forest would be 10^{15}, equivalent to the number of connections in the human brain!

Denton added:

Even if only one hundredth of the connections in the brain were specifically organized, this would represent a system containing a much greater number of specific connections than in the entire communications network on Earth.

Or consider this. Denton argues:

The capacity of DNA to store information vastly exceeds that of any other known system; it is so efficient that all the information needed to specify an organism as complex as man weighs less than a few thousand millionths of a gram. The information necessary to specify the design of all the species of organisms which have ever existed on the planet, a number according to G.G. Simpson of approximately one thousand million, could be held in a teaspoon and there would still be room left for all the information in every book every written.

These facts raise the obvious question: *could any sort of purely random process ever have assembled such systems in the time available?*

Denton's book, Evolution: A Theory in Crisis, is must reading for anyone who loves God and pursues truth!

Timeless Truth

I praise you because I am fearfully and wonderfully made;
your works are wonderful, I know that full well.

Psalm 139:14

A Timely Insight into . . .

Charles Allen described Knute Rockne as "The greatest football coach of all time." One of Rockne's ground rules for recruiting players for Notre Dame was this:

> "I will not have a boy with an inferiority complex.
> He must believe he can accomplish things."

I suppose that only a fool would cross swords with "the greatest football coach of all time." Well, here goes! When God does His recruiting, He is not looking for someone who believes that he or she can accomplish great things. He is looking for someone who believes that God can accomplish great things through a man or a woman, and a boy or a girl.

We live in an "age of psycho paganism," argues popular author and wise-cracking philosopher, Peter Kreeft. His indictment may seem unjust, but perhaps we should try it on for size.

If there is one message all our psychopagan prophets insist on, it is that we must love ourselves. But if there is any one message that Jesus and all His saints insist on, it is that we must deny ourselves. In Christ's psychology, the absolute oxymoron is "St. Self."

Let's quit all this nonsense about believing in yourself. What difference does it make whether you believe in you? If you want to make a difference, try believing that God believes that He can use you.

That will get you started! And that will get you across the finish line!

Believing in yourself may cause you only to cross the line— into pride!

Timeless Truth

But we have this treasure in jars of clay to show that this all-surpassing power is from God and not from us.

2 Corinthians 4:7

A Timely Insight into . . .

George Washington Carver, the son of a black slave woman, became a chemist in the agricultural department at the Tuskegee Institute in Alabama. From his countless experiments, Carver's research developed 300 products derived from peanuts. Products like flour, coffee, dyes, plastics, wood stains, soap, and cosmetics were developed from the humble peanut. Here was Carver's own explanation for his success in milking the peanut for more than it is worth:

When I was a boy, I said to God, "God, tell me the mystery of the universe." But God answered, "That knowledge is reserved for me alone." So I said, "God, tell me the mystery of the peanut." Then God said, "Well, George, that's more nearly your size." And He told me.

Timeless Truth

If any of you lacks wisdom, he should ask God,
who gives generously to all without finding fault,
and it will be given to him.

James 1:5